P9-CFA-959

LUCILE L. MORGAN

20630

ENT'D OCT 3 0 2007

LUCILE L. MORGAN LIBRARY
541 Ross St.
Heflin, Alabama 36264

Happy Quilts

Happy Quilts

Cheerful Projects to Brighten Your Home

Cheryl Fall

LUCILE L. MORGAN LIBRARY
541 Ross St.
Heflin, Alabama 36264

STERLING PUBLISHING CO., INC.
NEW YORK

Text and cover photographs by Nancy Palubniak

Edited by Isabel Stein

We have made every effort to ensure the accuracy and completeness of the patterns and instructions in this book. However, we cannot be responsible for human error, or for the results when using materials other than those specified in the instructions or for variations in individual work. Neither the author nor the publisher assumes any responsibility for any damages or losses incurred that result from the use of this book.

A special thank you to the following manufacturers for sharing their products: Coats & Clark, Singer Sewing Company, Pellon, and Fairfield Processing.

Library of Congress Cataloging-in-Publication Data
Fall, Cheryl.
    Happy quilts : cheerful projects to brighten your home / by Cheryl Fall.
        p.   cm.
    Includes index.
    ISBN 0-8069-0754-1
    1. Quilting—Patterns.   2. Quilted goods.   I. Title.
TT835.F334   1994
746.46—dc20   94-30298
                                                                 CIP

10 9 8 7 6 5 4 3 2 1

Published by Sterling Publishing Company, Inc.
387 Park Avenue South, New York, N.Y. 10016
© 1994 by Cheryl Fall
Distributed in Canada by Sterling Publishing
% Canadian Manda Group, One Atlantic Avenue, Suite 105
Toronto, Ontario, Canada M6K 3E7
Distributed in Great Britain and Europe by Cassell PLC
Villiers House, 41/47 Strand, London WC2N 5JE, England
Distributed in Australia by Capricorn Link (Australia) Pty Ltd.
P.O. Box 6651, Baulkham Hills, Business Centre, NSW 2153, Australia

Printed and bound in Hong Kong

All rights reserved

Sterling ISBN 0-8069-0754-1

Contents

Preface 7

TECHNIQUES, SUPPLIES, AND TOOLS

Basic Techniques

Machine Piecing 11

Pressing Techniques 12

Appliqué Basics 13

Applying Piping and Other Trim 15

Basting the Quilt Layers 16

Machine- and Hand-Quilting 16

Clipping Curves and Corners 18

Making Your Own Binding 18

Applying the Binding 20

Hanging a Quilt 21

The Necessary Supplies

Fabric 22

Thread 22

Batting Products 23

Lace and Trim 23

Fusible Interfacing or Webbing 23

Stabilizers Used in Machine Appliqué 23

Tools and Tips

Care of the Sewing Machine 24

Scissors and Rotary Cutters 25

Marking Pens and Pencils 25

The Seam Ripper 25

Quilting Hoops and Frames 25

Other Useful Items 26

THE PROJECTS

1. Coffee Klatch Wall Hanging 29

2. Little Houses Kitchen Set 37

3. Sunflowers Quilt and Place Mat 44

4. Baby's Butterflies 53

5. Ships at Sea Baby Quilt and Pillow 63

6. Around-the-Square Lap Quilt 74

7. Rows of Roses Wall Hanging and Pillow 80

8. Confetti Four-Patch Lap Quilt 86

9. Birthday Banner 91

10. Watering Can Wall Hanging 96

11. Paper Dolls Wall Hanging 102

12. Stepped Star Quilt 107

13. Birdie's Little Abode Wall Hanging and Pillow 113

14. Wind Song Lap Quilt and Runner Set 121

15. Grape Cluster Apron and Bag Set 128

Quilting Patterns 136

Index 143

Useful Tables 144

 # Preface

Bright, happy, and fun best describes the quilts and other projects featured in this book. You'll find quilts that use traditional piecing techniques, as well as some featuring machine appliqué, and a fun technique known as the "pen stitch," which uses a permanent pen to give the effect of hand quilting. This technique has been so well received by my students that I just couldn't resist including it in the book. You may use it on virtually any of the appliqué projects in this book, if you wish. Once you've tried this technique, I guarantee you'll be hooked.

The projects themselves range from wall hangings and banners to lap-size quilts and table accessories. Feel free to use the appliqué motifs on your own project ideas, and remember, all of the machine appliqué patterns can be easily adapted to hand-appliqué by adding seam allowances to all edges of the appliqués.

Happy quilting!
Cheryl

Techniques, Supplies, and Tools

Basic Techniques

Machine Piecing

After cutting all of the necessary pieces, machine stitch the pieces together, with their right sides facing, using a ¼-inch seam allowance (see Fig. 1). Always use a neutral-colored thread; however, if there is too much contrast in the fabrics to use a neutral thread, choose a thread that is one shade darker than the *lightest* fabric used in the project.

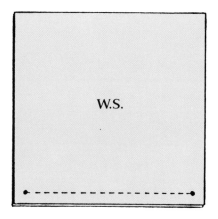

1. *Machine or hand piecing.*

All of the quilt templates in this book use a ¼-inch seam allowance, and it is included in all of the instructions for piecing, as well as in the given measurements for all of the pieces whose patterns aren't given. If you are unsure if you can stitch an exact ¼-inch seam allowance when you are machine-piecing, measure ¼-inch from the right side of the needle and place a small piece of masking tape at the ¼-inch mark on your machine. Use this tape as your stitching guide.

To save time, chain piece when possible. Align all pairs to be stitched with right sides of fabric facing, and feed them through the machine one pair at a time, butting but not overlapping the units. Continue to stitch the units, without cutting the thread between units (Fig. 2). When you have sewn all of the units, clip the connecting stitches apart.

When hand-piecing, join two pieces at a time using size 7 or 8 (sharp) hand-sewing needles. Use the running stitch and take

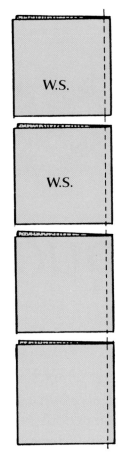

2. Chain stitching multiple units to save time.

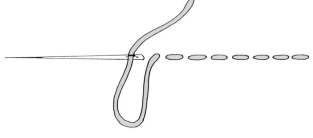

3. The running stitch, used for hand piecing.

the seam. Open out the pieces so that the seam allowances are pressed towards the darker fabric and press again, setting the seam allowance into position (Fig. 4a).

To save time, try to set aside groups of units to be pressed; this way you won't feel like you're constantly bouncing from the machine to the ironing board. Also, don't use an iron with an "automatic shutoff" feature if you plan on sewing for any length of time—you'll be constantly re-

approximately 10 stitches per inch (Fig. 3). Backstitch at the ends to secure the thread.

Pressing Techniques

Get into the habit of *always* pressing your seam allowances after stitching. Always be sure to press with a *dry* iron. The use of steam can stretch and distort the pieces, and you need to keep them as accurate as possible for proper piecing. To press properly, press along the seam line *before* opening out the joined pieces. This will set

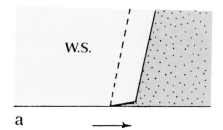

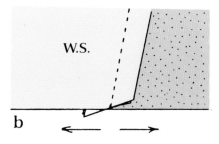

*4. Pressing seam allowances. **a:** Press single seam allowance towards the darker fabric. **b:** Press intersecting seam allowances in opposite directions.*

starting the thing. When pressing pieces with intersecting seam lines, press each set of seam allowances in opposite directions (Fig. 4b). This reduces the bulk you will be quilting through later.

Appliqué Basics

An appliqué is a cutout decoration of fabric that is laid on and sewn to a larger piece of fabric. Machine appliqué is both fun and easy once you know the proper method of stitching. If you've had problems in the past, try it again—you won't be disappointed.

After cutting the base fabric on which your appliqués will be sewn, lightly trace the entire block design onto the right side of the base fabric with a water-soluble pencil. This will help you with the placement of the appliqués when you secure them to the base fabric.

Next, trace the reversed appliqué shapes onto the paper side of the fusible interfacing. Roughly cut out the shape and fuse it to the wrong side of the appliqué fabric. Remember that the appliqué will be facing in the *opposite* direction after it has been fused and cut out (Fig. 5), so reverse any patterns that aren't symmetrical before you trace them onto the webbing.

After fusing the appliqué to the interfacing, cut out the appliqué shape through both layers. No seam allowance is necessary for machine appliqué.

To sew the appliqué on, place a piece of stabilizer slightly larger than the appliqué design against the *wrong* side of the base fabric (Fig. 6). This will keep your machine from shoving the fabric through the hole

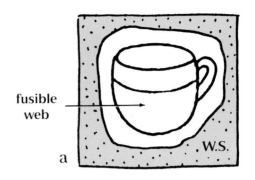

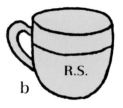

fusible web

5. *a:* The appliqué facing the opposite direction, traced onto fusible webbing and fused to the wrong side of the appliqué fabric. *b:* The cut-out appliqué.

stabilizer

6. The stabilizer is cut slightly larger than the base fabric and is pinned to the wrong side of the fabric.

in the throat plate as you stitch, and it will keep your stitches from puckering. *Do not eliminate this step, as you'll be asking for trouble!* Set the sewing machine to a medium-width satin stitch, and thread the machine with thread that matches the color of each individual appliqué. Use a neutral thread in the bobbin. Before you start, do a test or sample on scrap fabric. Does the bobbin thread pull to the top? If so, you have incorrect tension on your machine. Loosen the upper tension slightly, which should correct the problem. If it doesn't, replace your needle—a dull needle or one with burrs can cause your machine to stitch incorrectly. Use a size 9 or 11 universal point needle. Make any other necessary adjustments before moving to the actual appliqué.

The satin stitch should entirely cover the raw edges of each of the appliqués. The left swing of your needle should be in the appliqué itself, and the right swing should be in the base fabric (Fig. 7).

To appliqué at right-angled corners, stop the needle at the outer point of the appliqué. Swing the base fabric around to the next position and continue stitching. If the appliqué piece comes to a narrow point, taper the width of your stitching by adjusting the width of the satin stitch as you stitch along the point (Fig. 8).

To appliqué a curved or circular piece, you will need to stop stitching and pivot the fabric frequently to get a nice, smooth curve. To do this on an outside curve, stop the needle in the base fabric and turn the work slightly. Repeat until you have completed stitching the entire curve. To stitch an inside curve, pivot the work in the same manner, but stop the needle in the appliqué piece instead (Fig. 9).

For hand appliqué, trace the appliqué shape onto the wrong side of the fabric, and cut out the shape *adding ¼ inch seam*

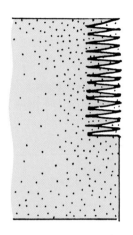

7. The correct stitch for machine appliqué.

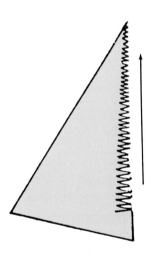

8. Taper the width of the satin stitch at the points.

allowances all the way around it as you cut. Fold the seam allowances to the wrong side of the fabric and hand stitch the appliqué to the base fabric, using an invisible stitch, with matching thread (Fig. 10).

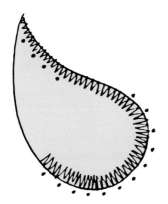

9. *Pivot points for stitching curved pieces.*

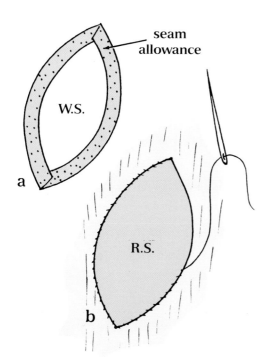

10. *Hand-appliqué technique.* **a:** *Seam allowances folded to the wrong side of the appliqué.* **b:** *Stitching the appliqué to the background fabric.*

Applying Piping and Other Trim

Applying piping or other decorative trims is very simple. To pipe a straight edge, simply lay the piping or lace against the fabric, having the raw edge of the piping or the gathered edge of the lace even with the raw edge of the fabric, and baste it in place using a ¼-inch seam allowance.

When you get near the corner, stop stitching ¼ inch from the edge. Make a small clip in the seam allowance of the piping, but do not cut through to the area containing the cord itself (Fig. 11a). Continue basting the piping along the next

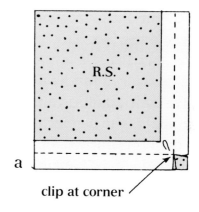

a

clip at corner

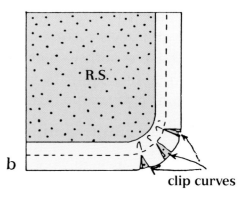

b

clip curves

11. *Basting piping to a rectangle* **(a)** *and to a curved edge* **(b)**.

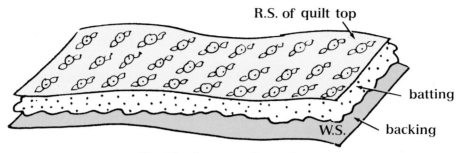

R.S. of quilt top

batting

W.S. backing

12. The layers of a quilt.

edge. To pipe a curved edge, clip into the seam allowance every ½-inch or so to make the trim lie flat (Fig. 11b). Remember, do not cut past the seam allowance and into the piping itself! Continue basting. The piping is usually sewn in at the same time the two pieces of fabric it is in between are joined.

Basting the Quilt Layers

Your quilt is basically a sandwich: the "bread" is the backing fabric and the quilt top, and the filler is the batting (Fig. 12). Lay out the quilt on your work surface with the right side of the backing fabric face down; tape it to your work surface. Center the batting over the wrong side of the backing fabric, and center the quilt top, face up, over the batting. Thread-baste by hand or pin-baste the layers together with large safety pins, every 3 or 4 inches. Always start basting at the center of the quilt and work your way out to the sides, smoothing the layers as you baste (Fig. 13).

Machine and Hand Quilting

The sample projects in this book have all been machine-quilted. You may choose to hand-quilt your project if you wish, however. To machine-quilt, loosen the upper

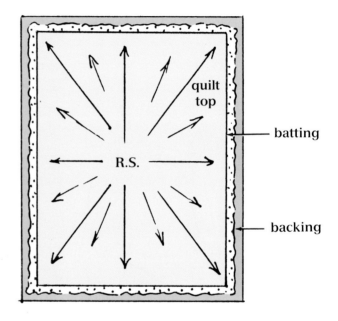

quilt top

batting

R.S.

backing

13. Basting the quilt; work from the center outwards.

tension of the machine very slightly, and thread the top of the machine with a neutral thread or clear nylon monofilament. Load the bobbin with thread to match the backing fabric. Set the machine stitch length to approximately 8 stitches per inch.

For best results, use a walking foot, also known as an *even feed foot*. These normally do not come with your machine as standard equipment, but they can be pur-

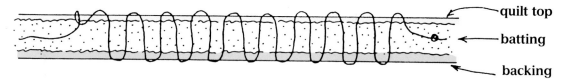

14. *A cross-section of the quilt, showing the quilting stitch, with the knot buried in the batting.*

chased at many sewing machine stores for your particular brand—and they are relatively inexpensive. This foot will feed the layers of your quilt together evenly, allowing you to machine-quilt without puckers, which might normally occur if you used a standard foot. When you use a standard foot, the feed dogs tend to push the bottom layer of the quilt through faster than you can hand-push the top layers of the fabric through, resulting in puckering.

You may choose to machine-quilt in free-motion style. To do this, use a darning foot and lower your feed dogs. You will now have to maneuver the fabric through the machine by hand, but you will be able to make curves and swirls! The possibilities here are endless.

To hand-quilt, secure the basted quilt into a hoop or quilting frame. Start with a small needle like a quilter's between-sized needle, threaded with a length of quilting thread. Knot the end of the thread. Pull the thread through the top layer of the quilt and into the batting; tug the thread to pull the knot through the top layer and bury it in the batting (Fig. 14). You don't want any knots showing on the top of the quilt or the backing. Quilt with small running stitches (Fig. 3).

For best results with both hand- and machine-quilting, stitch around the appli-

15. *Two quilting patterns.* ***a:*** *Criss-cross quilting lines.* ***b:*** *Echo quilting.*

qués and stitch along all of the seamlines. Stitch again ¼ inch from the seamlines and the appliqué edges. Depending on the type of batting you have chosen (see the section on batting), you may need to continue and heavily quilt any open areas with a filler stitch such as criss-crossed lines (Fig. 15a) or echo quilting (Fig. 15b), quilting ¼ inch from each previous line of quilting until the area is filled (Fig. 15).

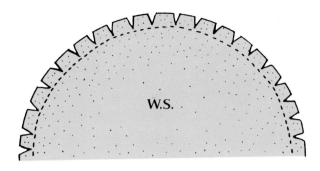

16. Clipping seam allowances on curves.

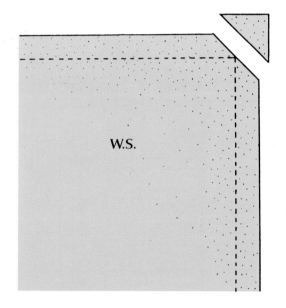

17. Clipping corners of seam allowances.

Clipping Curves and Corners

This terribly important step is often overlooked when making a project, resulting in curved areas that will not lie flat, or corners that are rounded. Clipping the curves of the seam allowance on a rounded project (Fig. 16) will give you a nice, flat curved edge, and it will also eliminate the bulk of the seam allowance in a project. This neatens its appearance and makes it easier to quilt as well. You certainly

wouldn't want an oval place mat that curls towards your place setting, or one with bulky edges. Clipping the corners off the seam allowances of a squared project (Fig. 17) reduces the bulk at the corners, allowing the corners to lie flat and have a nicely pointed appearance. Always clip close to but not through the stitching lines.

Making Your Own Binding

I have used prepackaged binding throughout the projects for this book. However, you can easily make your own binding. To make your own binding, cut 2-inch-wide strips of fabric along the bias (at a 45° angle to the selvage) of the fabric (Fig. 18a). All of the strips must have 45° angles at the ends. Stitch the ends of the strips together as shown in Figure 18c. Clip off the little tails of the seam allowance after stitching the strips together and press the seam allowances open. For the first fold of the tape, fold both sides of the strip to the center, with right side of fabric out, and press (Fig. 18d). Next, fold the strip down the center (Fig. 18e) for the center fold; this results in a double-fold bias binding (Fig. 18f).

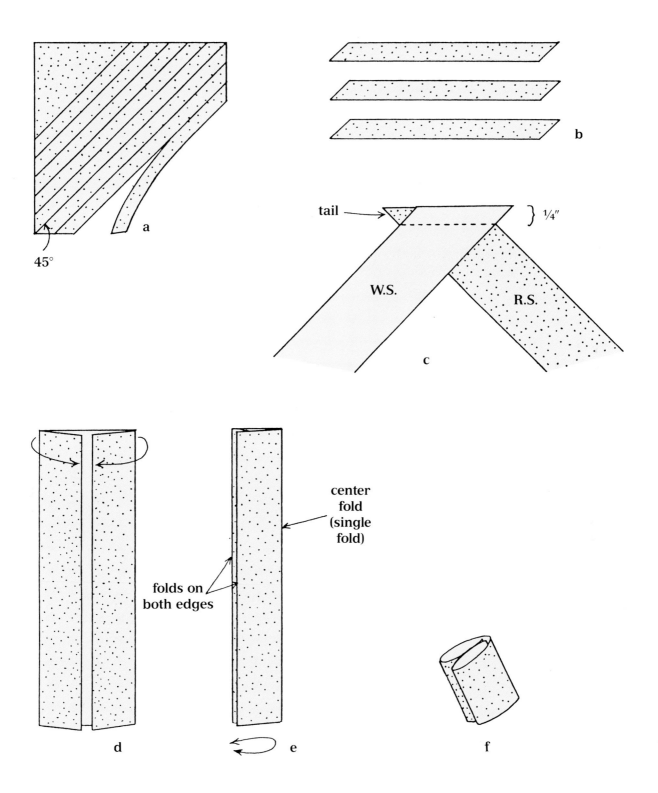

18. *Making double-fold bias binding.* ***a:*** *Cutting strips at a 45° angle.* ***b:*** *The cut strips.* ***c:*** *Joining two strips.* ***d:*** *Folding the sides in to meet in the center.* ***e:*** *Folding the strip in half so the two previous folds end up at the left.* ***f:*** *Cross-section of bias binding.*

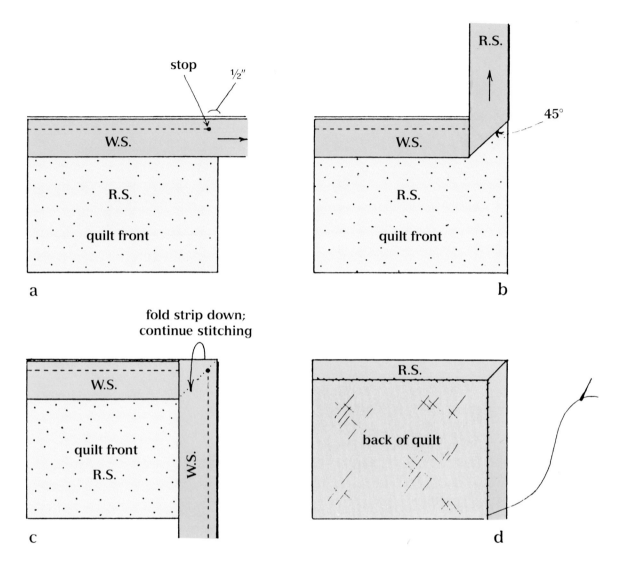

19. *Applying bias binding.* **a:** *Stitch up to ½-inch (for extra-wide binding) from the first corner; with raw edges aligned and right sides of material facing; then stop and cut the thread.* **b:** *Fold the bias strip up at a 45° angle.* **c:** *Fold the bias strip down, with the top fold aligned with the first raw edge.* **d:** *After turning the unattached long raw edge of the bias binding over to the quilt back, slipstitch it in place with a ½-inch seam allowance turned under.*

Applying the Binding

Unfold the premade or purchased binding and place one raw edge of the binding against the outside edge of quilt on the quilt front, with right sides of the fabric facing and edges aligned. Stitch along the top crease of the binding to within ½ inch of the corner (Fig. 19a). End off the thread. At the corner, fold the binding up, aligning the side of the binding with the side of the quilt (Fig. 19b). Fold the binding down, having the resulting fold of the binding even with the top edge of the quilt, and continue stitching (Fig. 19c). Repeat the procedure for each side of the quilt and to turn the corners. Fold the loose edge of the binding to the opposite (backing) side of the quilt, turn under a hem, and hand-stitch it in place to secure the binding, making sure your stitches are not visible on the opposite side of the quilt (Fig. 19d).

Hanging a Quilt

To hang a quilt, you can create a fabric tube attached to the back side of the quilt near the top. To make one:

1. Cut a strip of fabric 8 inches wide; cut the length of the strip one inch shorter than the width of the quilt. For example, if your quilt is 30″ × 30″, your strip would be 8″ × 29″.

2. With right sides of fabric facing, fold the tube in half down its length and stitch along the long edge, ¼ inch from the double raw edges (Fig. 20a). Turn the tube right-side out.

3. Turn the ends of the tube in ¼ inch, press, and secure them with stitching (Fig. 20b).

4. Press the tube so that the seam is in the center of the flattened area.

5. Slipstitch the tube to the backing side of the quilt near the top by hand (Fig. 20c). Insert a rod into the tube for hanging.

6. Suspend the rod from curtain rod hooks or thin wires and S-hooks from the wall or moulding.

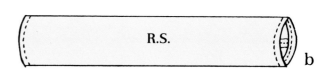

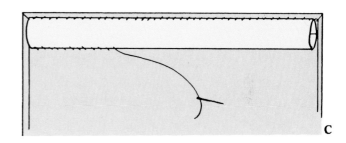

*20. **a:** Fold and stitch the strip to form a tube. **b:** Turn right-side out and hem the edges. **c:** Slipstitch the tube to the back of the quilt, near the top.*

The Necessary Supplies

Fabric

I recommend using only 100% cotton fabrics. Cotton is very easy to work with and it will not slide as you stitch, as a blend or a polyester would. Cotton is also very forgiving if you happen to make a mistake. Blends may also be used when necessary, but make sure they have a higher percentage of cotton than other fibers. Blends have a tendency to slip and slide, or to fray when washing, so always try to use cotton.

Prewash and press all fabrics before beginning a project. Replace any fabrics that may continue to "crock" or "bleed" (lose their dye) after washing, as the dye may spoil your completed project after it is washed. Prewashing also removes any sizing or starchy finishes that are added to the fabric by the manufacturers; this makes the fabric easier to handle. Also, be sure your fabrics are on-grain after washing (Fig. 21).

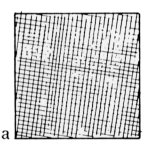 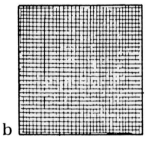

21. a: Off-grain fabric. b: On-grain fabric.

Thread

I prefer to use all-purpose thread in piecing and quilting. However, I like to use special threads like rayon or metallics for machine appliqué. Rayon and metallics, however, are purely decorative and should not be used for any assembly.

You may also use cotton thread, but you'll have a better range of colors to choose from if you opt for all-purpose thread.

Batting Products

I used traditional-weight polyester batting or polyester fleece in the projects in this book. It is the most commonly available form of batting. When purchasing batting for a machine-made project, always read the package carefully. You will notice that the manufacturer gives recommendations as to the spaces between lines of quilting; these are very important. If you plan to do a minimal amount of quilting, choose a batting with a wider spacing ratio. If not, your batting will shift when you wash the finished item and it could become a lumpy mess.

Also, do not choose a high-loft or "fat" batting for hand or machine appliqué. These are meant for tied quilts and are very difficult to quilt through.

Quilt batting is normally sold by the pre-cut piece in a bag, or off a bolt by the yard. Fleece, which is a very dense form of polyester batting, is sold by the yard and should be used for place mats and runners, as it gives the finished piece a bit more stiffness than regular batting would.

Lace and Trim

Choose lace and trim that are of good quality. Stay away from those tables full of "bargain" laces, as they are rarely the bargain they appear to be. Shop wisely. This tip applies to thread and fabric as well.

Prewash your lace and trim by gently swishing them in warm sudsy water. Rinse them thoroughly and hang them up to dry. Prepackaged trims, such as binding and piping, do not require prewashing; the manufacturer has taken this step for you.

Fusible Interfacing or Webbing

When a project calls for fusible webbing, this means a paper-backed webbing. This can go by various brand names. It is sold by the yard or in prepackaged units at fabric stores.

Trace your appliqué patterns onto the paper side of the webbing (see Fig. 5) and fuse the roughly cut webbing shapes to the wrong side of the fabrics. Cut out the shapes, remove the paper backings, and fuse the unit in position on the base fabric. Follow the manufacturer's directions regarding iron heat and timing. See the Appliqué Basics section of the "Basic Techniques" chapter for more details.

Stabilizers Used in Machine Appliqué

It is very important to use stabilizer. If you ever attempted machine appliqué and became discouraged because your fabric became tangled in the hole in the throat plate of your sewing machine, it's because you didn't use stabilizer. Stabilizer is a stiff paper or fiber "fabric" that you place against the back side of your base fabric, to give the base fabric extra body and stability. Stabilizer is sold by the yard or prepackaged at fabric stores. You may also use scratch paper, such as typing paper, as stabilizer. After choosing a stabilizer, cut a piece of it that is slightly larger than the base fabric, and pin it to the wrong side of the base fabric at the corners. Now you may machine-appliqué without getting your fabric stuck in the hole, and the edges of the appliqués won't pucker.

Tools and Tips

Care of the Sewing Machine

Always keep your sewing machine in good working condition, especially if you plan to do any machine appliqué. Your sewing machine is like any other machine; like your car or your VCR, it needs to be cleaned and serviced once in a while. Regularly clean and oil your sewing machine. Cleaning removes the debris that can clog the feed dogs or jam the machine. Oiling keeps the machine running smoothly and *quietly*. A noisy machine is one in need of help!

Referring to your owner's manual, adjust the thread tension properly. The tension must be evenly balanced. I've run across so many students' machines that have had their bobbin tension tightened to the point to not being able to loosen it with a jack hammer (okay, maybe I didn't try a jack hammer, but it was darn tricky to loosen that screw!).

If you are still having trouble, adjust the tension as follows: To have a properly set bobbin tension, hold the bobbin case in your hand and slide the bobbin into it as if it were in the machine. Now, let go of the case while holding onto the end of the bobbin thread. If the case slides down to the floor, leaving you with a 4-foot tail of thread, your tension is too loose. If not, *gently* shake the thread and watch the bobbin case. If it doesn't go anywhere, your tension is much too tight! If it slips ever so slightly, you have nearly perfect tension.

Now replace the bobbin case and bobbin in the machine, and thread the machine with the same weight of thread used in the bobbin, but in a different color. Test sew a length of straight stitch on a doubled scrap of fabric and look at the resulting stitch. If the bobbin thread has been pulled to the top of the fabric, your upper tension is too tight. If the upper thread is pulled to the wrong side of the fabric, your upper tension is too loose. Adjust the upper tension so that the stitch becomes balanced.

If you have tried the steps given above and the tension is still awful, have it professionally serviced. It's worth it! You wouldn't neglect a tune-up on your car, would you?

Scissors and Rotary Cutters

Always use a nice sharp pair of scissors for cutting fabric—and use them only for this purpose. Label them FABRIC ONLY and use an older pair of scissors for cutting paper or other materials. Occasionally, nonquilting members of the family will try to use your fabric scissors for cutting paper or whatever. If this happens, throw a fit and hide those scissors where only you can find them! (Some people put out alternate scissors for general use.) Your scissors should not cause you any discomfort when cutting. If they do, you may need to have them sharpened and the joint oiled.

A rotary cutter with a self-healing plastic mat and a see-through plastic ruler are very handy tools for quilters. These may be used on the projects in this book that require pieces with straight edges, and for cutting border and sashing strips. As with scissors, make sure the rotary cutter's blade is sharp and that it is used only for cutting fabrics. If the cutter skips along the fabric as you cut, you probably need a new blade. ALWAYS cut away from you. Retract the blade when it's not in use. Keep the rotary cutter and all other sharp tools away from small children.

Marking Pens and Pencils

Always use water-soluble pens and pencils for marking fabrics. DO NOT use a #2 graphite pencil for marking fabric.

Fabric and quilting supply stores carry a large number of water-soluble marking instruments. You can also use tailor's chalk or a soap sliver. I prefer to use a quilter's marking pencil. You can buy quilter's pencils in different colors. Use a white, yellow, or silver pencil for marking dark-colored fabrics; use a blue, black, or silver pencil for marking light-colored fabrics. When in doubt, test your pencil on a scrap of fabric and then wash the fabric. The markings should wash away easily. You can use a light box to trace patterns onto fabric, if you have one available.

The Seam Ripper

No, I'm not a perfect stitcher, either! I always have several of these little wonders handy. Using one doesn't mean you can't stitch well—it means that you care enough about what you're doing to do it properly. Seam rippers tend to go dull after repeated use. Replace them as necessary. It's better to rip than to have a crooked quilt.

Quilting Hoops and Frames

Hoops and frames are used for hand-quilting. Quilting hoops are like embroidery hoops, only larger. They are available in several sizes and variations. A hoop or frame will keep your work taut as you quilt, which helps avoid puckering of the backing or top. For very large projects, a quilting frame is helpful and performs the same function. Quilting frames may be homemade or purchased, and come in a variety of sizes and styles.

Other Useful Items

Below is a list of other tools and supplies you'll probably need:

· Sewing machine needles (size 9 or 11 universal point for appliqué work and piecing)

· Straight pins

· Tracing paper

· Graph paper or other gridded paper for enlarging patterns

· Cardboard or plastic for cutting templates of patterns

· Thimbles for hand-sewing and quilting

· Embroidery thread for hand embroidery (see individual projects for colors)

· Needles for both hand sewing and machine sewing, including crewel embroidery needles, sharps, and betweens (short needles of sizes 5 to 11, used for hand quilting)

· A heavy plastic ruler

· A pen with waterproof ink for tracing designs on paper or cardboard

· See-through 45°–45°–90° triangle (12-inch size is good)

· Masking tape to make identifying tags for parts of quilts, etc., before they are assembled

· An iron

Consult the materials list of the project on which you will be working for any other necessities.

The Projects

Coffee Klatch Wall Hanging

Friends add a certain warmth and comfort to everyday life. Meeting friends for coffee is a true pleasure for me. Once a month, four of us try to meet at a local restaurant to exchange news of family, daily life, to lend a listening ear, or just to gossip. Needless to say, during an animated conversation, sometimes more coffee is spilled than we drink. This wall hanging would brighten a kitchen or dining alcove. Make it in colors that complement your decor. Finished size of wall hanging: 33" (width) × 24" (length).

Materials Required

· *¾ yard white solid fabric*

· *⅓ yard yellow solid fabric*

· *½ yard bright blue print fabric*

· *⅓ yard bright red print fabric*

· *⅓ yard each red solid and blue solid fabrics*

· *¼ yard tan solid fabric*

· *⅓ yard bright yellow print fabric**

· *All-purpose threads to match all of the fabrics*

· *35" × 26" piece of fabric for the backing*

· *35" × 26" piece of quilt batting*

· *1½ yards fusible transfer webbing*

· *4 yards of ½"-wide quilt binding (2" wide when opened) in the color of your choice; yellow print was used in the sample**

---

*If you want to make the binding out of the yellow print fabric, increase yellow print fabric to ⅔ yard.

Overview: The quilt center is made up of 5 appliquéd blocks, framed with a narrow border and a wide border (see Fig. 1–1). All piecing is done with ¼" seam allowances. Appliqué patterns are given without seam allowances, as they are not needed for machine appliqué; add ¼" seam allowances for hand appliqué.

Directions

1. From the white solid fabric cut 4 A blocks, each 7½" × 8½". Cut an 11½" × 16½" piece of white fabric for the center panel (B). Set them aside.

2. Cut the inner borders strips from the solid yellow fabric; two 1½" × 16½" C strips for the side inner borders and cut two 1½" × 27½" D strips for the upper and lower inner borders. Set these strips aside for later use.

3. From the bright red print cut 4 E squares, 3½" × 3½" each, for the corners of the outer borders. From the bright blue print: cut two F strips, 3½" × 18½" each, for the side outer borders; and cut two G strips, 3½" × 28½" each for the upper and lower outer borders.

4. Using the full-size appliqué patterns, trace 4 cups, 4 saucers, 4 spoons, and one complete coffeepot onto the paper side of the fusible interfacing (see the "Basic Techniques" chapter for appliqué techniques). *The patterns are given in reverse, but they will be facing the proper direction when they are fused to the blocks later on.* Cut the shapes out of the interfacing.

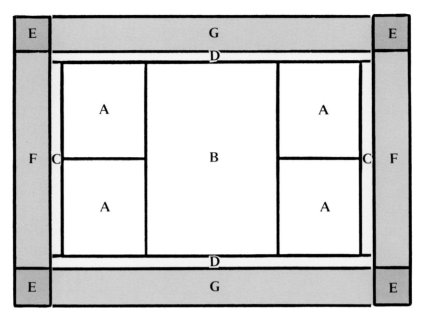

1–1. Construction diagram for the Coffee Klatch quilt.

5. Referring to the color photo for the correct fabrics, fuse the interfacing shapes to the wrong side of the various pieces of the blue, red, and yellow prints and solid fabrics, as shown in the photo. Cut out the shapes from the fabrics. Trace the coffee drips and the "spill" onto the remaining pieces of fusible webbing. Fuse them to the wrong side of the tan fabric and cut them out.

6. Position the cups, saucers, and spoons so they look tipped on the white 7½" × 8½" (A) blocks cut in Step 1, and fuse them in place (see photo). Fuse the coffeepot to center white panel cut in Step 1. Fuse one or two drips to each cup. Fuse the spill to the coffeepot as shown in Figure 1–2a.

7. Machine appliqué the fused pieces to the background blocks using a medium-width satin stitch and matching the threads to the fabrics.

8. Stitch two A blocks together, as shown in Fig. 1–3. Repeat with the remaining two A blocks. Stitch a unit of the two A blocks to each side of the center coffeepot panel. Press.

9. Referring to Figure 1–4, stitch the yellow C inner border strips (1½" × 16½") to the quilt center sides.

10. Stitch a yellow D border strip (1½" × 28") to the top and bottom of the unit made in Step 9.

11. Stitch the two blue G strips (3½" × 28") cut in Step 3 to the upper and lower edges of the quilt center, as shown in Figure 1–1. Stitch one red E square cut in Step 3 to the short ends of each of the two blue print F strips (3½" × 18½"). Stitch the side (F) borders with their

1–2. *Closeup of **(a)** the spill for the coffeepot, as it should be placed for fusing, and **(b)** one coffee cup and its drop.*

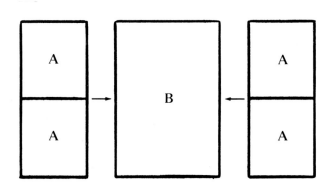

1–3. *Stitch two of the A blocks together for the side units. Repeat with the remaining two A blocks. Then stitch one side unit to each side of the center panel.*

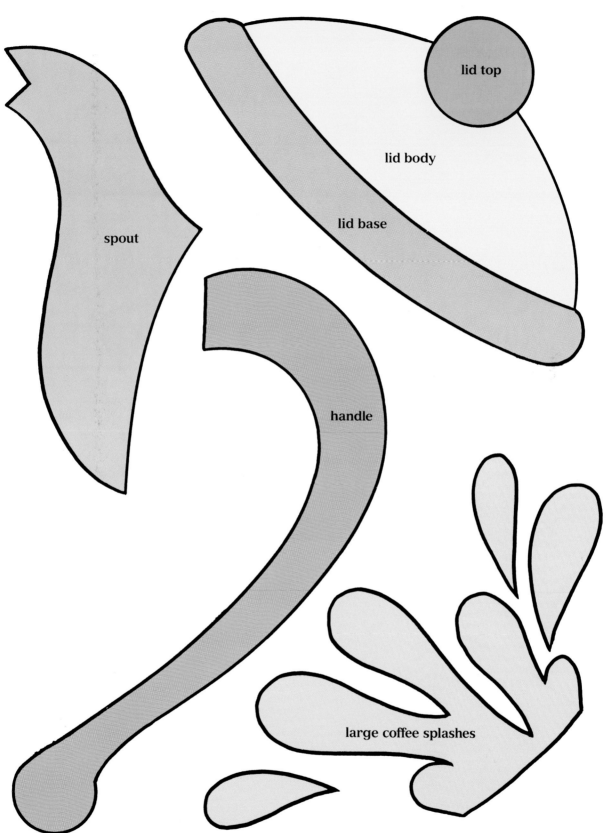

Templates for the coffeepot spout, lid, handle, and splashes. Templates are given in reverse; seam allowances are not included or needed for machine appliqué; add ¼" seam allowances for hand appliqué.

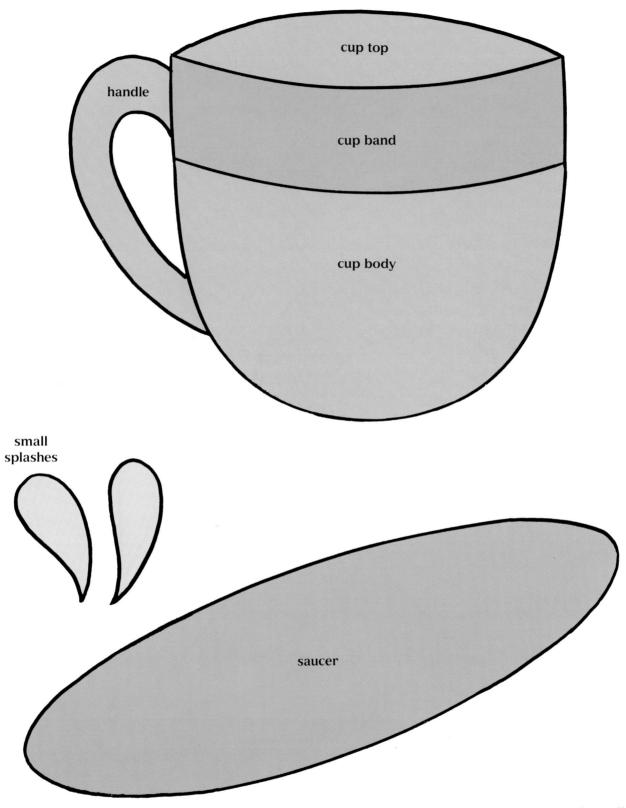

Templates for the cup, saucer, and small splashes. Templates are given in reverse. Seam allowances are not included for machine appliqué; add ¼″ seam allowances for hand appliqué.

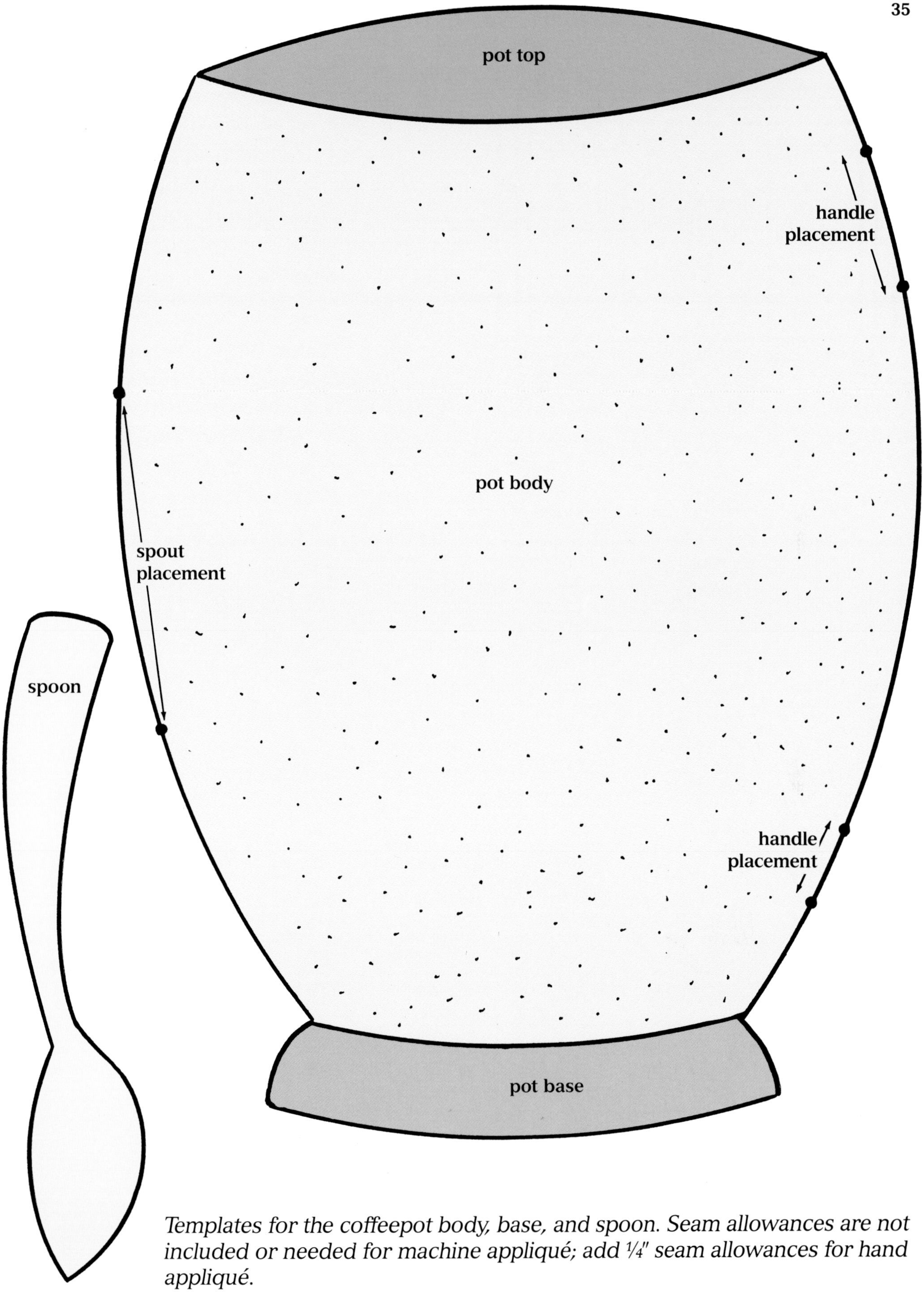

pot top

handle placement

handle placement

spout placement

spoon

pot body

pot base

Templates for the coffeepot body, base, and spoon. Seam allowances are not included or needed for machine appliqué; add ¼" seam allowances for hand appliqué.

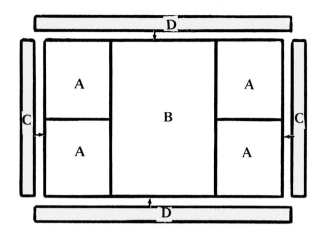

1–4. Stitch the yellow inner borders to the quilt center. Attach the C borders first.

attached corner units to the sides of the quilt center. Press. You now have a completed quilt top.

12. Lay the backing fabric face down on the floor or on a large table and tape it in place. Center the quilt batting over the wrong side of the backing and center the quilt top, right side up, over the batting. Hand or pin-baste the layers together.

13. Machine or hand-quilt as desired (refer to the "Basic Techniques" chapter if necessary). Baste ½" in from the raw edges of the quilt top all around the top when you are done quilting, and trim away the excess batting and backing.

14. Bind the quilt with the yellow binding to complete it.

Little Houses Kitchen Set

Materials Required

For Each Place Mat

· *14½" × 10½" piece of white fabric*

· *⅓ yard large-scale print fabric (for border)*

· *2 yards of black piping*

· *7" square of fusible webbing (interfacing)*

· *Scraps of the red, blue, and green print fabrics from the wall hanging*

· *16" × 20' piece of fleece or low-loft quilt batting*

· *16" × 20' piece of backing fabric of choice*

· *Thread (same as for the wall hanging)*

For the Wall Hanging

· *15½" × 13½" piece of white fabric*

· *¼ yard black fabric (for inner border)*

· *½ yard large-scale print fabric (for outer border)*

· *½ yard fusible webbing (interfacing)*

· *¼ yard each: red, green, and blue fabrics, either solid or small prints*

· *25" × 27" piece of backing fabric of choice*

· *25" × 27" piece of quilt batting*

· *3 yards black bias binding, ½" wide finished size (2" wide when opened)*

· *1 spool black all-purpose thread*

· *1 spool black buttonhole thread*

For Each Coaster

· *6" × 7" piece of fleece or low-loft batting*

· *6" × 7" piece of fusible webbing*

· *6" × 7" piece of backing fabric*

· *Scraps of red, blue, and green prints from the above projects*

· *Threads as for the above projects*

Bright colors and a simple pattern make this set fun to make. Using a machine stitch that mimics a hand-made blanket stitch speeds up the assembly of these projects; however, directions are also given for hand buttonhole stitch, if you prefer. If you are unable to locate buttonhole-weight thread, carpet thread or pearl cotton makes a good substitute. *Finished size of place mat: 18½" (width) × 14½" (length). Finished size of wall hanging: 23" × 25". Finished size of coaster: 5" × 6".*

Directions

Note: The buttonhole thread is used only for the blanket stitch. Use the all-purpose thread for all of the assembly and basting. Piecing is done with right sides of fabric facing and ¼" seam allowances. Appliqué patterns are given without seam allowances, which are not needed for machine appliqué. (Add ¼" seam allowances to appliqué patterns for hand appliqué.)

For Each Place Mat

1. Trace the house pattern onto the paper side of the fusible interfacing, being sure you have drawn all the lines. Cut the interfacing into four sections: the

House template, full-size; seam allowances are not included. (Add ¼″ seam allowances if you will hand appliqué.)

roof, side, and front of the house, and the heart. Fuse the house front to the blue fabric; the house side to the green fabric; the roof and heart to the red fabric. Cut out the shapes from their fabrics, and fuse one complete set to the lower right section of a 14½″ × 10½″ piece of white fabric (see Fig. 2–1 for positioning; position the house so that it is about 2″ in from the raw edges of the white fabric.)

2. From the large-scale print, cut 4 border strips, 2½″ × 14½″ each. Referring to

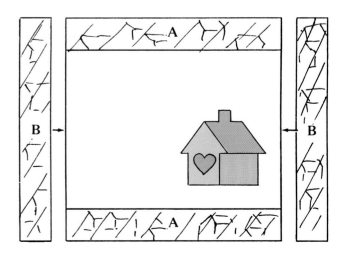

2–1. Stitching the borders to the place mat center.

Figure 2–1, stitch one border strip (A) to the upper and one to the lower edge of the white 14½″ × 10″ place mat center, using black, all-purpose thread. Stitch the remaining two border strips (B) to the sides of the unit just made. Press.

3. Baste the fleece or quilt batting to the wrong side of the place mat front, trimming away the excess fleece after basting. Baste the piping around the edges of the place mat front, having the raw edges of the piping even with the raw edges of the place mat. (See the "Basic Techniques" chapter for more information on applying piping.)

4. Place the place mat front and backing fabrics together, with right sides of fabric facing, and stitch together ¼″ in from the raw edges of the place mat, leaving a 6″ opening along one long side for turning. Trim away the excess backing fabric and clip the corners of the seam allowances. Turn the place mats right-side out and hand-stitch the turning opening closed.

5. Pin-baste through all of the layers of the place mat, securing the layers to keep them from shifting during the appliqué/quilting process—you will be appliquéing and quilting at the same time.

6. Set your sewing machine to a stitch that mimics a hand-sewn blanket stitch. Referring to Figure 2–2, stitch around the edges of each section of the house with the blanket stitch, using the *buttonhole thread*. (Note: you may do the blanket stitching by hand, if you

2–2. Using the blanket stitch to attach an appliqué. The stitches follow around the edges of the appliqués.

prefer. Use a double length of buttonhole thread in an all-purpose sewing needle. See Figure 2–3 for the hand blanket stitch).

7. Using all-purpose thread and a machine straight stitch, stitch in the ditch along the seam line bordering the white center section to secure the border areas.

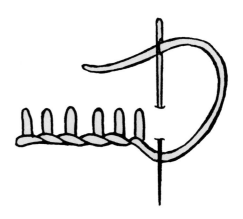

2–3. Stitching diagram for hand-sewing the blanket stitch.

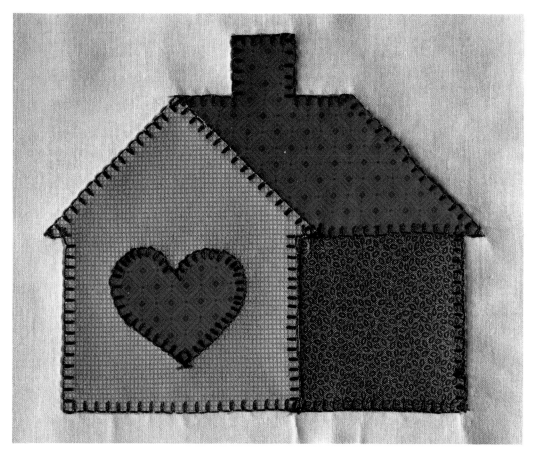

Closeup of place mat, showing blanket stitch.

Coasters

1. Trace the house pattern to the paper side of the 6″ × 7″ piece of fusible interfacing, including all the lines. Cut the interfacing into 4 pieces—the roof, side, and front of the house, and the heart. Fuse the interfacing pieces to the wrong sides of their various fabrics (see photos for colors).

2. Baste the 6″ × 7″ fleece to the wrong side of the 6″ × 7″ piece of backing fabric. Fuse the house pieces to the *fleece* and baste *very close* to the *outer* edges of the house. Trim away the excess backing fabric and fleece close to the raw edges of the house.

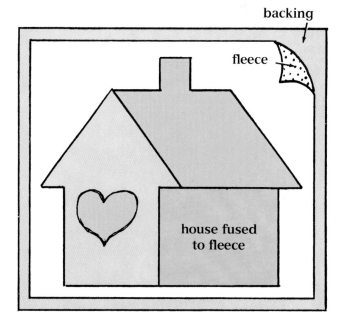

2–4. Center the fleece over the wrong side of the backing fabric. Fuse the appliqués to the fleece.

3. Machine satin-stitch around the *outer edges* of the house, using black all-purpose thread.

4. Using the buttonhole thread, blanket-stitch around the unstitched seams of the appliqué to complete the coaster.

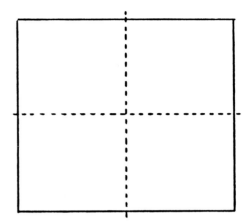

2–5. *Fold the white fabric into quarters and press. Mark along the creases to divide the fabric into quarters.*

Wall Hanging

1. Fold the 15½" × 13½" piece of white fabric into quarters and press. Draw a line with a chalk pencil along each fold to mark the quarters of the white piece, as shown in Figure 2–5.

2. Trace 4 reversed houses onto the paper side of fusible interfacing, including all the lines. Cut the interfacing into 4 sections: roof, heart, house side, and house front. Fuse these to the wrong side of their respective fabrics (see photo). Cut the shapes out of the fabrics. Assemble and fuse one house to the center of each quarter of the white fabric rectangle folded in Step 1.

3. From the solid black fabric, cut 4 inner border (A) strips, 1½" × 15½" each. Stitch one strip to the top and bottom of the white rectangle. Stitch the remaining 2 A strips to the sides of the unit (see Figure 2–6). Press.

4. From the large-scale print fabric, cut two 4½" × 17½" C strips, and stitch them to the top and bottom sides of the quilt center. Cut two 4½" × 23½" D strips from the same print, and stitch them to the sides of the unit (Fig. 2–6). Press.

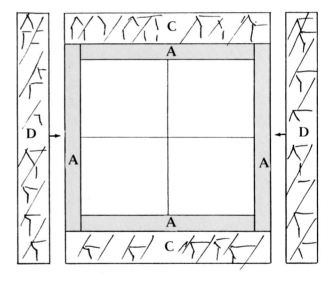

2–6. *The quilt top, showing the inner and outer borders.*

5. Lay the backing fabric face down on your work surface and tape it in place. Center the quilt batting over the backing fabric, and center the quilt top, face up, over the batting. Hand-baste or pin-baste the layers together. To quilt, stitch in the ditch along the seam lines and along the fold marks (made in Step 1) dividing the white area. Using the black all-purpose thread, baste ½″ in from the raw edges of the quilt top.

6. Using the black buttonhole thread, machine blanket-stitch the appliqués, as for the place mats.

7. Trim away the excess batting and backing and bind the finished quilt with the black bias binding.

Sunflowers Quilt and Place Mat

Materials Required

For the Quilt

· *1¼ yards natural-colored solid fabric*

· *½ yard large-scale floral print fabric (for border)*

· *¼ yard medium green small-scale print fabric (for leaves)*

· *¼ yard dark green solid fabric (for leaves)*

· *¾ yard bright yellow print fabric*

· *½ yard dark brown print fabric (for sunflower centers and the inner border)*

· *¼ yard rust print fabric*

· *2 yards of fusible webbing*

· *44″ × 44″ piece of backing fabric of choice*

· *43″ × 43″ piece of quilt batting*

· *All-purpose threads to match all of the fabrics*

· *4 yards of bias binding that has a finished width of ½″ (2″ wide unfolded)*

You can almost feel the Mediterranean breezes when you look at this set. The bright yellow flowers will put a smile on your face each time you see them, and the projects are actually *very* easy—you can have a set of place mats made in just a few hours! *Finished size of the quilt: 40″ × 40″. Finished size of place mat: 16″ diameter, from point to point.*

For Each Place Mat

· *17″ × 17″ square of bright yellow print fabric*

· *9″ × 9″ square of dark brown print fabric*

· *One 9″ × 9″ and one 17″ × 17″ piece of fusible webbing*

· *17″ × 17″ square of backing fabric of choice*

· *17″ × 17″ piece of fleece or low-loft quilt batting*

· *Threads to match the yellow and brown fabrics*

· *½ yard ¼″-wide green satin ribbon for trim (optional)*

Directions

All construction is done with ¼″ seam allowances. Appliqués don't require seam allowances for machine appliqué; add ¼″ seam allowances for hand appliqué.

For the Quilt

1. From the natural solid fabric, cut 9 squares, each 10½″ × 10½″. Fold each square into quarters and press it to mark the center. (Fig. 3–1).

2. From the dark brown print cut two A strips, 1½″ × 30½″ each, and two B strips, 1½″ × 32½″ each. These will be your inner borders. Set them aside for now.

3. From the quilt appliqués trace 9 quilt flowers, 9 flower centers, and 36 leaves onto the fusible webbing, using the templates. Roughly

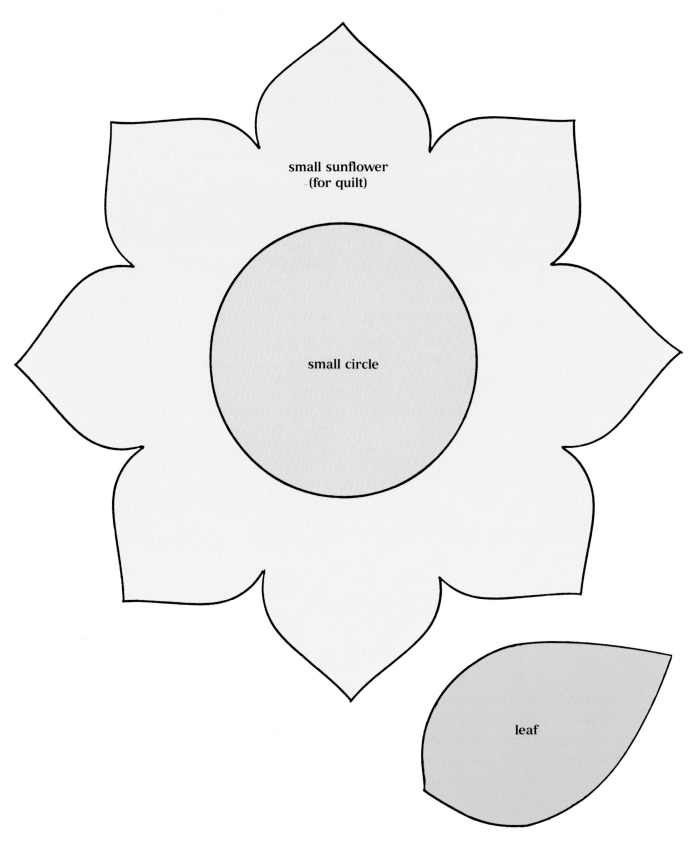

small sunflower
(for quilt)

small circle

leaf

Full-size quilt flower, circle, and leaf templates. Seam allowances are not included or needed for machine appliqué. Add ¼" seam allowances for hand appliqué.

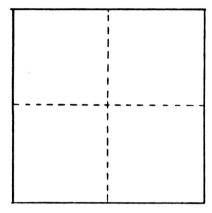

3–1. Fold each square into quarters and press to mark center.

3–2. Appliqués fused to a square.

cut out the shapes from the webbing. Fuse the flowers to the wrong side of the bright yellow print fabric. Fuse half of the webbing leaves to the wrong side of the dark green solid fabric and the remaining half to the wrong side of tne medium green print fabric. Fuse 5 of the quilt flower centers to the wrong side of the dark brown print and the remaining 4 flower centers to the wrong side of the rust print. Cut out all of the shapes. Fold each flower in quarters to find its center.

4. Fuse one flower, one flower center, two dark green leaves, and two medium green leaves to each of the blocks cut in Step 1, centering the flower on the center of each block (Fig. 3–2).

5. Machine-appliqué the pieces to the blocks, using the matching threads and a medium-width machine satin stitch.

Closeup of appliqué.

6. Arrange the blocks in 3 rows of three on your work surface; place the flowers with the dark brown centers at the corners and at the center (Fig. 3–3a). Using natural-colored thread and a ¼" seam allowance

a

b

3–3. *a:* *Arrange the blocks on your work surface.* *b:* *Stitch 3 blocks together in a row.*

throughout the assembly, stitch the blocks together in 3 rows of 3 blocks each (Fig. 3–3b). Stitch the 3 rows together to form the quilt center. Press.

7. Stitch the A strips cut in Step 2 to the top and bottom of the quilt center. Stitch the B strips to the remaining two sides (Fig. 3–4). Press the seam allowances towards the brown fabric.

8. From the large-scale print fabric, cut two C strips, 4½″ × 32½″ each, and stitch one strip to the top and one to the bottom of the quilt center. Cut two D strips, 4½″ × 40½″ each, and stitch them to the remaining two sides (Fig. 3–5). Press.

3–4. *Stitching the inner borders to the quilt center.*

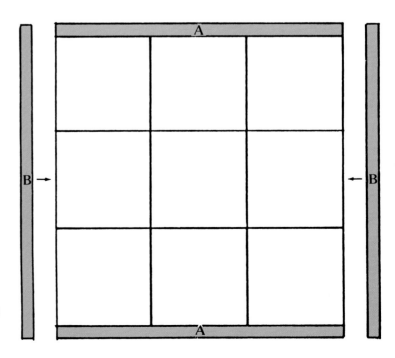

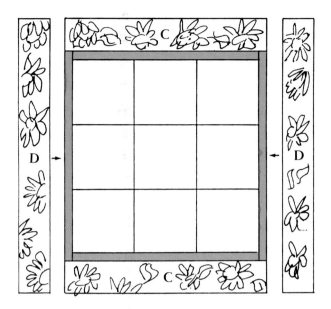

3–5. Stitching the outer borders to the quilt center

9. Lay the backing fabric face down on a clean floor or other work surface. Center the batting over the backing, and center the quilt top over the batting. Hand-baste or pin-baste the layers together. Machine-quilt as desired. *

10. Baste close to the raw edges of the quilt top all around, and trim away the excess batting and backing. Bind the edges of the quilt with the bias binding to complete the quilt (see binding instructions in the "Basic Techniques" chapter).

For a Place Mat

1. Fold the 17" square of fusible webbing into quarters and mark the fold lines with a pencil. Now mark the diagonal center lines to further divide the square into eighths (Fig. 3–6a). Trace the ⅛th flower template for the place mat onto

*See the quilting pattern section at the back of the book for optional quilting patterns.

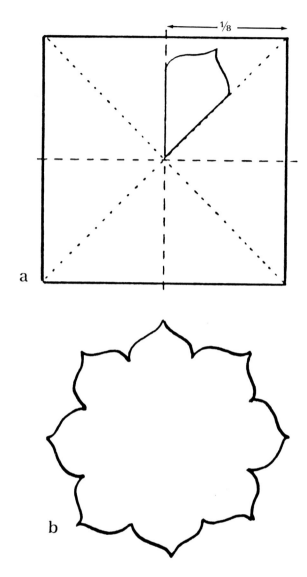

3–6. a: Mark out eighths on the square of fusible webbing. Trace the ⅛th flower template onto each eighth of the square. b: The complete flower shape.

each eighth of the fusible webbing, with the template's center aligned to the square's center. Then fuse the webbing to the wrong side of the 17" square of yellow fabric. Cut out the flower shape along the OUTER edges only (Fig. 3–6b).

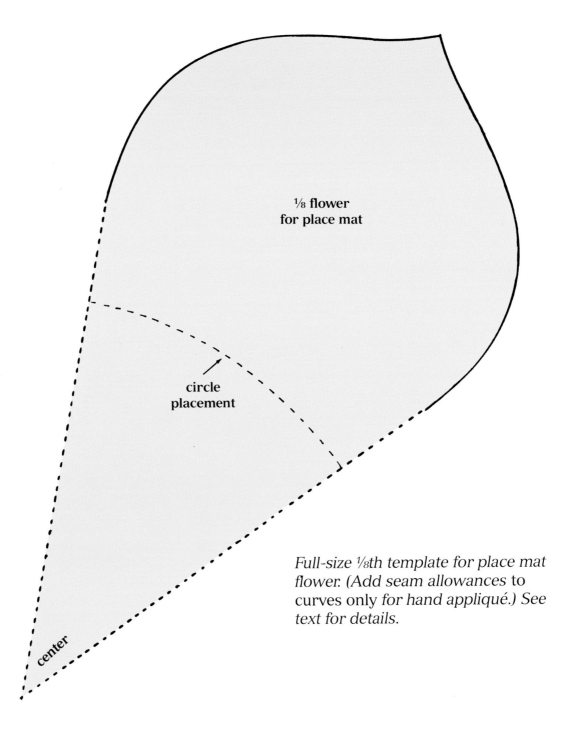

⅛ flower
for place mat

circle
placement

center

*Full-size ⅛th template for place mat
flower. (Add seam allowances to
curves only for hand appliqué.) See
text for details.*

2. Fold the 9″ square of fusible webbing in
half and mark the center line. Trace one
circle half onto the fusible webbing; flip
it over and trace again to make a
complete center circle (see Fig. 3–7).
Fuse the webbing circle to the wrong
side of the 9″ square of dark brown

fabric and cut the circle out. Fuse the circle to the right side of the yellow flower cut in Step 1, centering the circle on the flower.

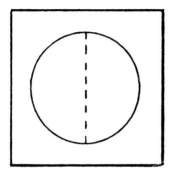

3–7. Trace the flower center onto fusible webbing.

3. Place the 17″ square of backing fabric face down, and center the 17″ square of fleece over the backing. Center the flower from Step 2 on the fleece. Baste VERY close to the raw edges of the flower and cut away the excess backing and fleece (Fig. 3–8).

4. Machine satin-stitch along the raw edges of the flower, using yellow thread. Satin-stitch along the edges of the brown flower center with brown thread. Straight-stitch the petal lines (Fig. 3–9).

5. Tie the length of ribbon into a bow and tack it to the flower, near the edge of the flower center, as shown in the photograph.

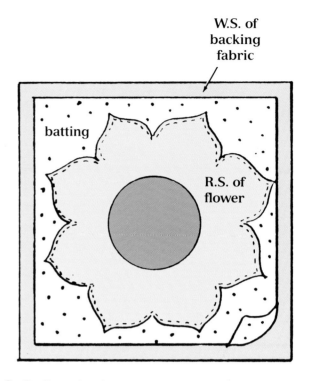

W.S. of backing fabric

batting

R.S. of flower

3–8. Lay the fleece over the wrong side of the backing fabric. Fuse the flower face up on the fleece. Baste close to the raw edges of the flower. Cut out the flower shape after basting.

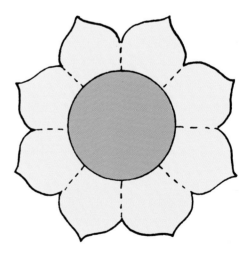

3–9. Stitch as shown by the dotted lines to indicate the petal divisions.

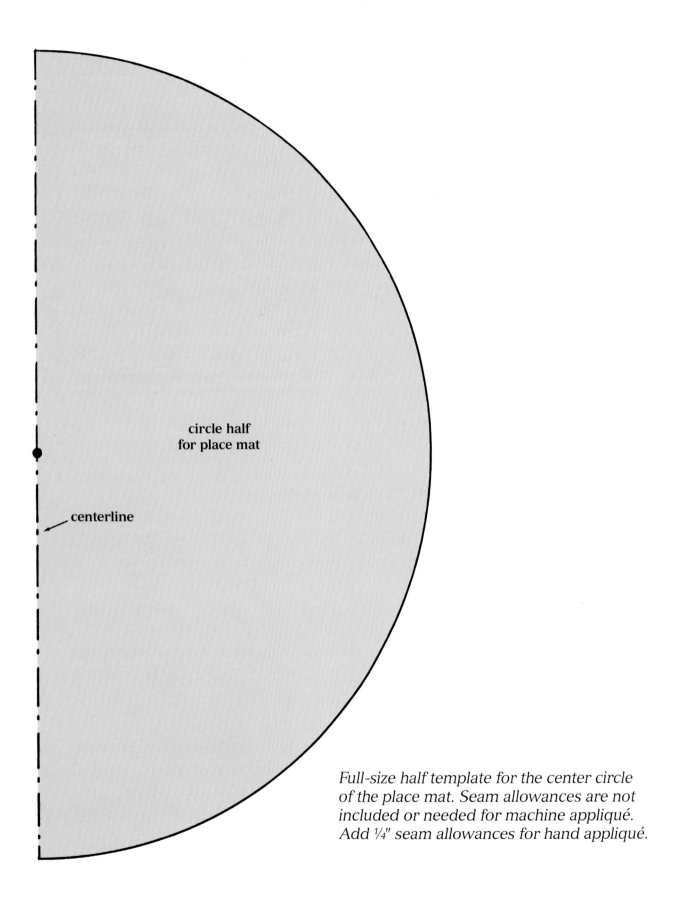

circle half
for place mat

centerline

Full-size half template for the center circle of the place mat. Seam allowances are not included or needed for machine appliqué. Add ¼″ seam allowances for hand appliqué.

Baby's Butterflies

Materials Required

For the Quilt
- *1½ yards white fabric*
- *¾ yard bright blue solid or small-scale blue print (for blue border and butterfly)*
- *1 yard red small-scale print fabric (for red border and butterfly)*
- *2 yards total of at least 8 additional assorted bright-colored printed fabrics*
- *⅛ yard black fabric*
- *44″ × 44″ piece of fabric of choice for the backing*
- *44″ × 44″ piece of quilt batting*
- *4 yards of ½-inch wide bias binding (2″ wide when unfolded)*
- *2½ yards of fusible webbing (18″ wide)*
- *Threads to match all the fabrics*
- *Black 6-strand embroidery floss (for embroidering antennae) and embroidery needle*

Bright colors and lively prints give this baby set character (however, you may substitute pastels if you prefer). Be sure to include washing directions if you're giving this as a gift. *Machine wash cold: tumble dry on low. Finished size of baby quilt: 41″ × 41″. Finished size of bib: Approximately 10″ × 12″.*

For Each Bib
- *11″ × 13″ piece of white fabric*
- *11″ × 13″ piece of backing fabric of choice*
- *10″ × 10″ piece of fabric for the butterfly wings*
- *Scraps of 2 additional fabrics for body and circles on wings*
- *11″ × 13″ piece of fleece or low-loft quilt batting*
- *11″ × 13″ piece of fusible webbing*
- *2 yards of ½″-wide bias binding (2″ wide when unfolded)*
- *Threads to match fabrics*
- *Black 6-strand embroidery floss*

Directions

All construction is done with ¼″ seam allowances and right sides of fabric facing. Appliqués don't require seam allowances for machine appliqué. Add ¼″ seam allowances for hand appliqué.

For the Quilt
1. Set aside the ⅛ yard of black fabric; you will only use this fabric for the sashing corners. From the white fabric, cut 9 squares, each 9½″ × 9½″.

2. From the ½ yard of blue fabric cut 2 A strips, 2½″ × 31½″ each, and cut two B strips, 2½″ × 35½″ each. From the yard of red fabric cut 2 C strips, 3½″ × 35½″ each, and 2 D strips 3½″ × 41½″ each. Set aside these blue and red strips for the inner and outer borders.

4–1. Trace one wing onto interfacing; reverse the pattern and trace the other wing.

3. Trace 9 butterfly wings onto the paper side of fusible webbing, using the wing pattern. Reverse the pattern and trace an additional 9 wings (Fig. 4–1). Trace 9 butterfly bodies and 36 wing circles onto the paper side of fusible webbing also, using the templates.

4. Fuse one webbing wing and one reversed webbing wing to the wrong side of the leftover red fabric (left after you cut the red border strips). Do the same with a piece of the leftover blue fabric that remained after cutting the blue border strips. Fuse one webbing wing and one reversed webbing wing to the wrong sides of 7 more fabrics from your assortment of bright colors.

5. Fuse the webbing butterfly bodies to the wrong sides of 9 fabrics. Fuse 36 wing circles to the wrong sides of 9 fabrics (4 to each fabric). Cut out all of the shapes from the fabrics.

6. Fuse one complete butterfly—one wing, one reversed wing of the same color, one body, and 4 wing circles (all circles of the same color)—to each of the white blocks cut in Step 1, referring to the color photo for inspiration if necessary. Fig. 4–2 shows all pieces fused to a block. Note that the butterflies are angled on the blocks, not straight up and down.

7. Transfer the markings for the antennae to each block from the pattern.

8. Machine-appliqué the pieces to the blocks using a medium-width machine satin stitch and threads that match the fabrics.

4–2. Fuse the pieces of the butterfly to each block, slightly at an angle. Vary position from block to block (see photo).

9. Hand-embroider the antennae in stem stitch using 2 strands of the black 6-strand embroidery floss in the needle (Fig. 4–3).

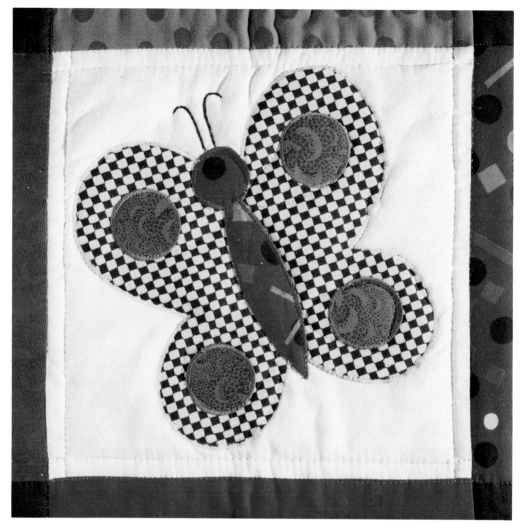

Closeup of block, showing machine appliqué.

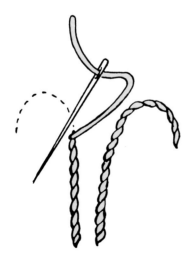

4–3. Embroider the antennae in stem stitch.

10. From all of the fabrics with the *exception* of the black, the white, and the blue fabric used to cut the inner borders, cut a total of twenty-four 1½″ × 9½″ strips for the block sashing. From the black fabric, cut sixteen 1½″ × 1½″ squares.

11. Referring to the construction diagram (Fig. 4–4), and using ¼″ seam allowances for all of the assembly work, stitch 4 sashing strips and 3 blocks together, alternating, to make a

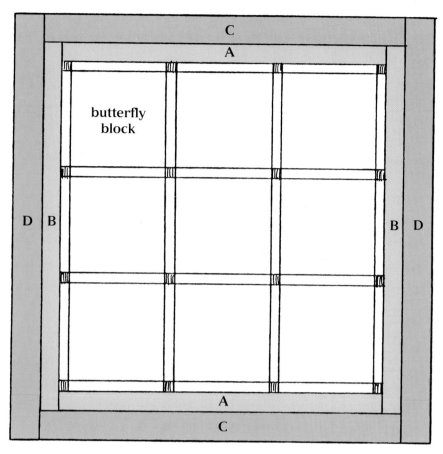

4–4. *Construction diagram for Baby's Butterflies.*

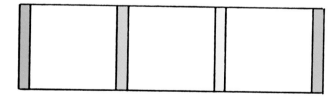

4–5. *Stitch 3 blocks, alternating with 4 sashing strips, to make a row.*

4–6. *Stitch 3 sashing strips, alternating with 4 small black squares, to make a long sashing strip.*

row (Fig. 4–5). Make 2 more rows the same way. Set them aside.

12. Stitch 3 sashing strips together, alternating with the 1½" black squares cut in Step 10, to make a long pieced sashing strip (see Fig. 4–6). Make 3 more long sashing strips the same way.

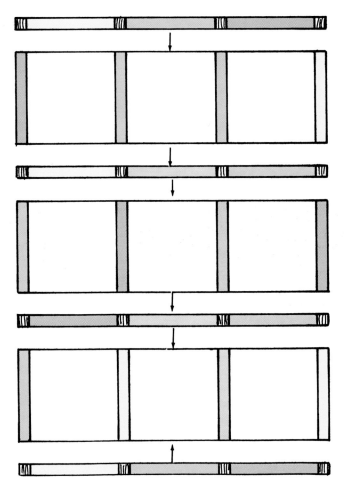

4–7 Join the rows and long sashing strips to make the quilt center.

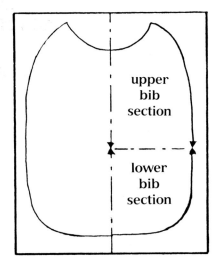

4–8. Trace the bib half-pattern, centered, onto the white fabric. Reverse the pattern and trace the other side.

baste or pin-baste the layers together. Machine- or hand-quilt, as desired.

16. Baste ¼″ in from the raw edges of the quilt top, all around the top. Trim away any excess batting and backing.

17. Bind the quilt with the bias binding sewn with matching thread.

13. Sew a long sashing strip above, below, and between the rows (Fig. 4–7) to assemble the quilt center.

14. Stitch the border strips cut in Step 2 to the quilt center. First attach the short A borders to the top and bottom of the quilt center; then add the side A borders. Repeat the process with the B borders (see Fig. 4–4 for reference).

15. Lay the backing fabric face down on your work surface and center the batting over the backing. Center the quilt top over the batting and hand-

For a Bib

1. Fold the 11″ × 13″ rectangle of white fabric in half lengthwise and press. Tape the two pieces of the bib pattern together and trace the right half of the pattern, with center lines aligned, on the right of the white rectangle. Flip the pattern over and trace it, reversed, to the left of the centerline (Fig. 4–8). Do not cut out the bib shape yet, however.

2. Trace two butterfly wings, one reversed, onto the paper side of fusible

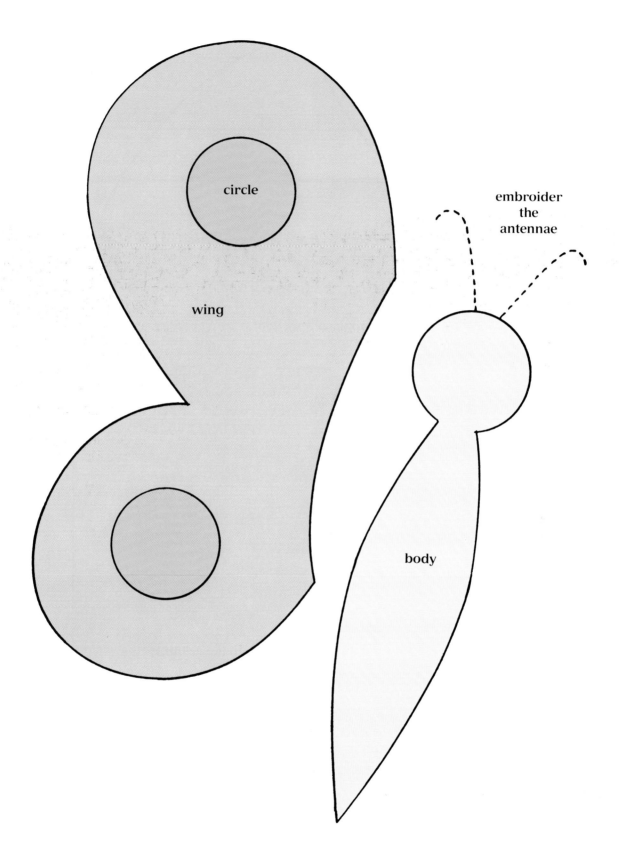

circle

wing

embroider
the
antennae

body

*Full-size butterfly wing and body templates. Seam allowances
are not included.*

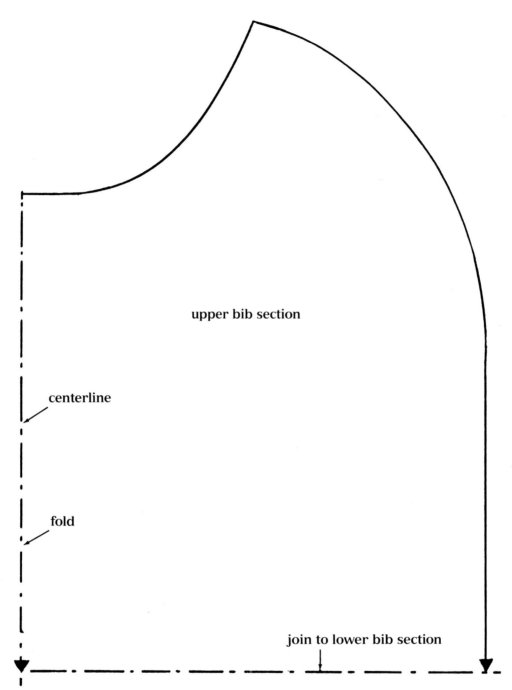

Full-size pattern for upper bib section. Attach to lower bib section and trace on fabric; reverse on centerline and trace again. Seam allowance = ¼".

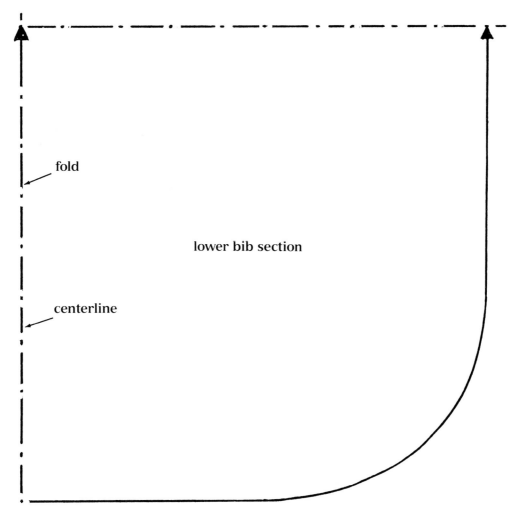

Full-size pattern for lower bib section.

webbing. Then fuse them to the wrong side of the 10″ square of butterfly wing fabric, and cut out the wings. Trace the butterfly body and circles onto webbing also, and cut them out. Fuse the body and the circles to the wrong sides of the scrap fabric colors you choose. Cut out all of the appliqué pieces from their fabrics, and fuse them, centered, onto the bib fabric (Fig. 4–9). Machine-appliqué the pieces in place, and embroider the antennae as for the quilt butterflies.

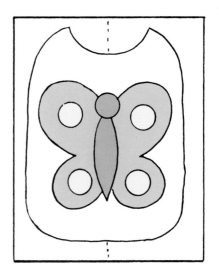

4–9. Fuse and appliqué one butterfly to the white fabric.

3. Lay the 11″ × 13″ piece of backing fabric face down and center the fleece or batting over the backing. Center the appliquéd white rectangle over the fleece. Machine-stitch about ¼″ in from the bib outline all around the bib. Cut out the bib shape close to but not through the stitching.

4. Bind the neck edge of the bib with a 7″ length of the bias binding, trimming off the excess at the ends (Fig. 4–10). Measure 18″ from the end of the excess bias binding and mark the binding. Place this mark at one neck edge of the bib. Bind all around the bib starting at this point. When you have bound the whole bib, measure off 18″ of binding beyond the edge for a bib tie; clip off any excess binding (Fig. 4–11a). Machine-stitch along the length of the ties on their doubled edge to close them, tucking the raw edges of the binding under ¼″ at the short ends (Fig. 4–11b).

5. Machine- or hand-quilt the bib as desired.*

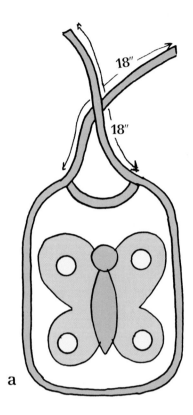

a

b

4–11. a. Bind the remaining edges of the bib, leaving an 18″ length unattached at the start of the binding and at the end of the binding on the opposite neck edge. *b.* Stitch detail of tie. Stitch along the double-folded edge of the bias binding to finish the ties, tucking the raw edge under at the end.

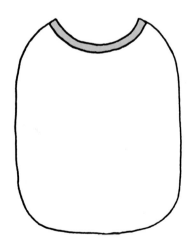

4–10. Bind the neck edge of the bib.

*See the quilting pattern section at the back of the book for optional quilting patterns.

Ships at Sea Baby Quilt and Pillow

Ahoy, Mates! Bundle your little sailors in this set and they'll sail right into dreamland! *Finished size of quilt: 34" × 38". Finished block size: 10" × 11½". Finished size of pillow: 15" × 15".*

Materials Required for Set

· *1¼ yards of blue print fabric (with small allover print)*

· *1½ yards white fabric*

· *1 yard red print fabric (with small allover print)*

· *¼ yard yellow fabric*

· *35" × 39" piece of quilt batting*

· *12-ounce bag of polyester fiberfill to stuff the pillow*

· *35" × 39" piece of fabric for the quilt backing*

· *15½" square of fabric for the pillow backing*

· *2 yards of white rickrack for pillow trim*

· *4 yards of ½"-wide white bias binding (2" width when unfolded) for the quilt*

· *White and yellow all-purpose thread*

· *½ yard fusible webbing*

Directions

All piecing is done with ¼" seam allowances and right sides of fabric facing. Star appliqués do not have seam allowances; add ¼" seam allowances around them for hand appliqué.

For the Quilt

1. From the blue print fabric cut 4 H strips, 2" × 31½" each, for joiner strips and short borders. Also from the blue print fabric cut two I strips, 2" × 38½" each, for long joiner strips. Set them aside.

2. From the red print fabric cut 6 strips, each 2" × 44". From the white solid fabric cut 6 strips, each 2" × 44". Set these 12 strips aside, as these will become the checkered areas of the quilt.

3. Make templates from the patterns by tracing the patterns A through G plus the small and large star onto paper. Be sure to note the direction of the grainlines on the patterns. Glue the patterns to lightweight cardboard and cut them out. Trace the pattern shapes onto the WRONG side of the fabrics, making certain that the paper side of the template is against the wrong side of the fabric and the lightweight cardboard side is facing you (the pattern is reversed). Cut out each piece. Using the chart below, cut out the correct numbers and colors of each piece (refer to Fig. 5–1):

   A: Cut 6 pieces from the blue print fabric
   A: Cut 6 pieces from the white fabric
   B: Cut 6 pieces from the blue print fabric
   B: Cut 6 pieces from the white fabric
   C: Cut 6 pieces from the blue print fabric

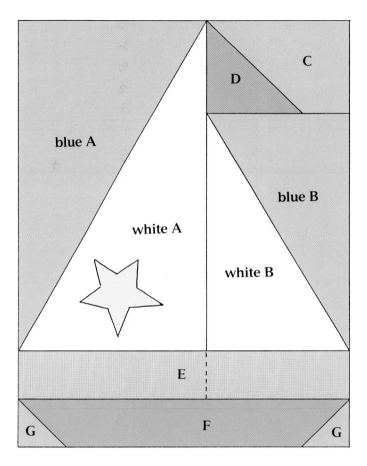

5–1. Construction diagram of quilt block, Ships at Sea Baby Quilt.

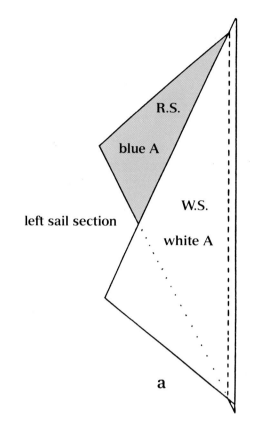

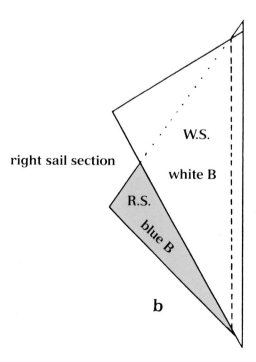

D: Cut 6 pieces from the red print fabric

E: Cut 6 pieces on folded fabric from the blue print fabric

F: Cut 6 pieces on folded fabric from the red print fabric

G: Cut 12 pieces from the blue print fabric

4. Stitch one white A piece to one blue A piece on their long sides (Fig. 5–2a) to make a left sail section. Repeat 5 times. Stitch one white B piece to one blue B piece (Fig. 5–2b) to make a right sail

5–2. Making the sail sections. **a:** Stitching the A pieces together for the left sail section. **b:** Stitching the B pieces together for the right sail section.

section. Repeat 5 times. Press the seam allowances towards the darker fabrics. Set them aside.

5. Stitch one red D piece to a blue C piece as shown in Fig. 5–3. Repeat 5 times. Press open with the seam allowances towards the blue fabric. These are the 6 flag sections.

6. Stitch one flag section to the top of each right sail section (made from the B pieces); see Figure 5–4. Set them aside.

7. Stitch one blue G triangle to each end of a red F piece; repeat 5 times to make 6 hull sections. (Fig. 5–5). Press them open, with the seam allowances

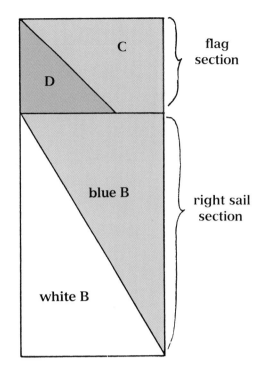

5–4. *Stitching the flag section to the right sail section.*

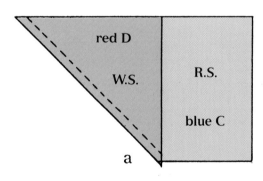

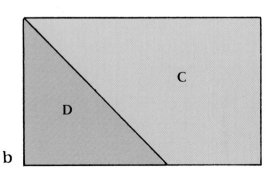

5–3. *a.* *Stitching the C and D sections together.* *b.* *The completed flag section.*

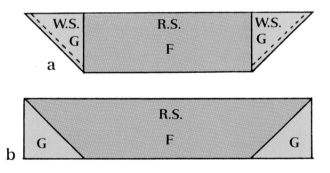

5–5. *a.* *Stitching G pieces to an F piece.* *b:* *The completed hull section.*

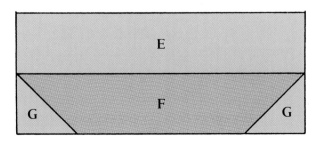

5–6. *Stitching the E piece to the hull section.*

towards the blue fabric. Stitch one blue E piece above each hull section (Fig. 5–6) for the lower block section.

8. Stitch the left sail section to the right sail section + flag section to make the upper portion of each block (Fig. 5–7, top). Stitch one upper portion to one lower block section to complete a block; repeat 5 times. Trace 6 small stars onto the paper side of fusible webbing and fuse them to the wrong side of yellow fabric. Cut them out. Fuse one star to each left sail section (see Fig. 5–1). Machine appliqué the stars in place, using a medium-width satin stitch and the yellow thread.

9. Stitch 3 of the pieced blocks from Step 8 together along their sides to make one row of blocks (Fig 5–8). Repeat with the remaining 3 blocks and press.

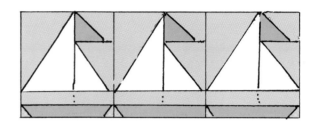

5–8. Stitching 3 blocks together.

10. Using the red and white 2″ strips you cut in Step 2, stitch a 3-strip red-white-red unit together along the long sides. Make another the same way (Fig. 5–9a). Then stitch a white-red-white 3-strip unit together (Fig. 5–9b) and make another the same way. Press the seam allowances towards the red fabric. Cut each resulting 3-strip into 2″ wide 3-piece units (each checkered square will eventually have a finished

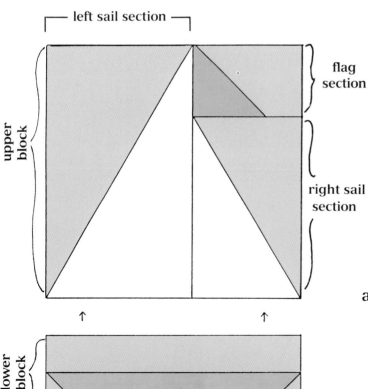

5–7. Stitching the upper block section to the lower block section to make a complete block.

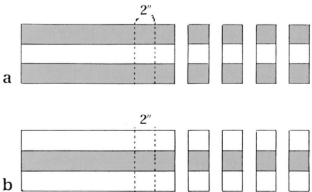

*5–9. Cutting the 3-strip units into 2″ wide sections. **a:** Red-white-red strip order. **b:** White-red-white strip order.*

Closeup of block showing quilt lines and pieces.

size of 1½″), cutting as many as possible from each long strip (Fig. 5–9). Stitch the 3-piece units together, alternating patterns, to make the checkered strips (Fig. 5–10a); each checkered strip should have twenty-one 3-piece sections (Fig. 5–10b). Reserve the remaining 3-piece units for the pillow.

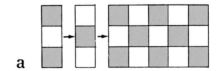

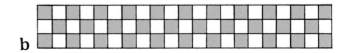

5–10. *Stitch 21 units together (a) to make a checkered strip (b).*

11. Referring to Figure 5–11, stitch the block rows, the checkered rows, and

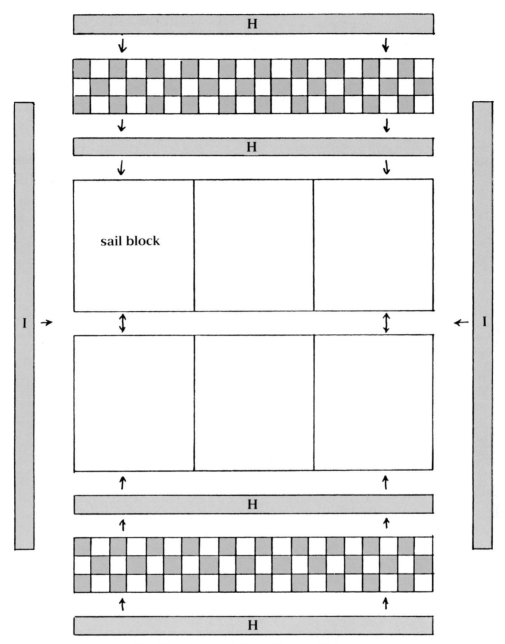

5–11. Assembling the quilt top.

the H joiner strips cut in Step 1 together as shown. Then stitch the I strips cut in Step 1 to the sides of the quilt top. Press.

12. Lay the backing fabric face down on your work surface and center the quilt batting over the backing. Center the quilt top over the batting and thread-baste or pin-baste the layers together. Machine- or hand-quilt as desired. * After quilting, baste around the raw edges of the quilt top, about ¼″ in, and trim away the excess batting and backing. Bind the edges of the quilt with the bias binding.

*See the quilting pattern section at the back of the book for optional quilting patterns.

For the Pillow

1. Using the leftover checkerboard sections from the quilt, stitch six 3-piece sections together to form a row, starting with a red-white-red unit (Fig. 5–12). Make another row starting with a white-red-white unit. Stitch the two rows together to make the pillow center.

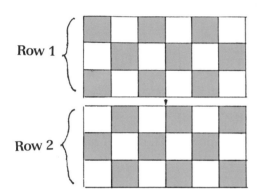

5–12. Stitch 6 alternating 3-unit sections together to form a row, starting with a red-white-red unit. Make another row starting with a white-red-white unit. Stitch the rows together to form the pillow center.

2. Trace one large star onto the paper side of fusible webbing and fuse it to the wrong side of the yellow fabric. Cut out the star and appliqué it to the center of the checkerboard square with a medium-width satin stitch and yellow thread.

3. From the blue print cut two A strips, 2″ × 9½″ each, and stitch them to two opposite sides of the pillow center (Fig. 5–13). Cut two B strips, 2″ × 12½″ each, and stitch them to the remaining sides.

4. From the red print, cut two C strips, 2″ × 12½″ each, and stitch them to two opposite sides of the pillow center. Cut two D strips, each 2″ × 15½″, and stitch them to the remaining two sides (Fig. 5–13). Press.

5. Baste the rickrack around the outer edges of the pillow top, with the side of the rickrack even with the raw edges of the pillow top, stitching along the center of the rickrack. Place the pillow top and the piece of backing fabric together, right sides facing, and machine stitch around the sides, leaving a 6″ opening along one side to turn the pillow cover.

6. Clip the corners and turn the pillow cover right-side out. Stuff the cover firmly with the fiberfill and hand-stitch the opening closed to complete the pillow.

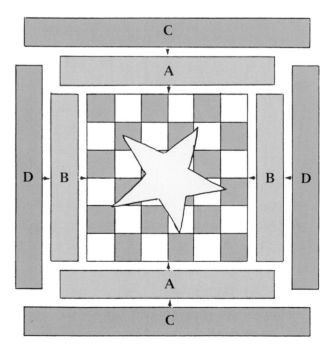

5–13. Adding borders to the pillow top.

Star appliqués for quilt block (small) and pillow (large). Seam allowances are not included or needed for machine appliqué. Add ¼" seam allowances for hand appliqué.

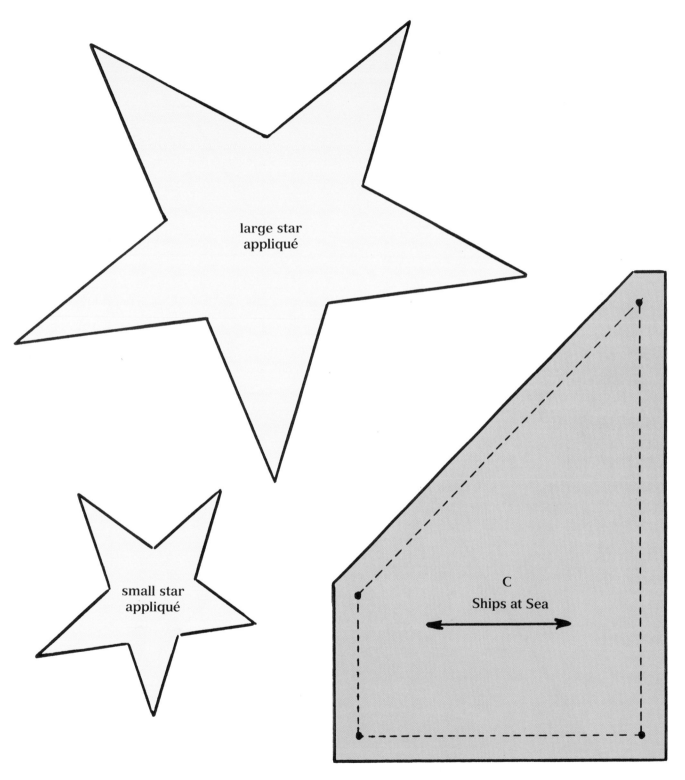

large star appliqué

small star appliqué

C
Ships at Sea

Full-size pattern for quilt block.

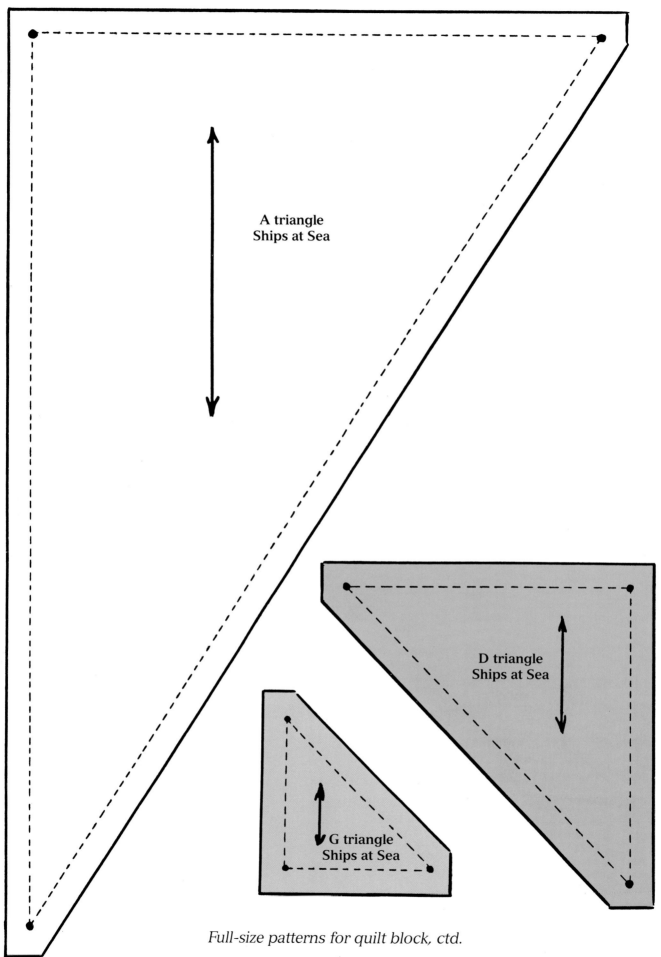

A triangle
Ships at Sea

D triangle
Ships at Sea

G triangle
Ships at Sea

Full-size patterns for quilt block, ctd.

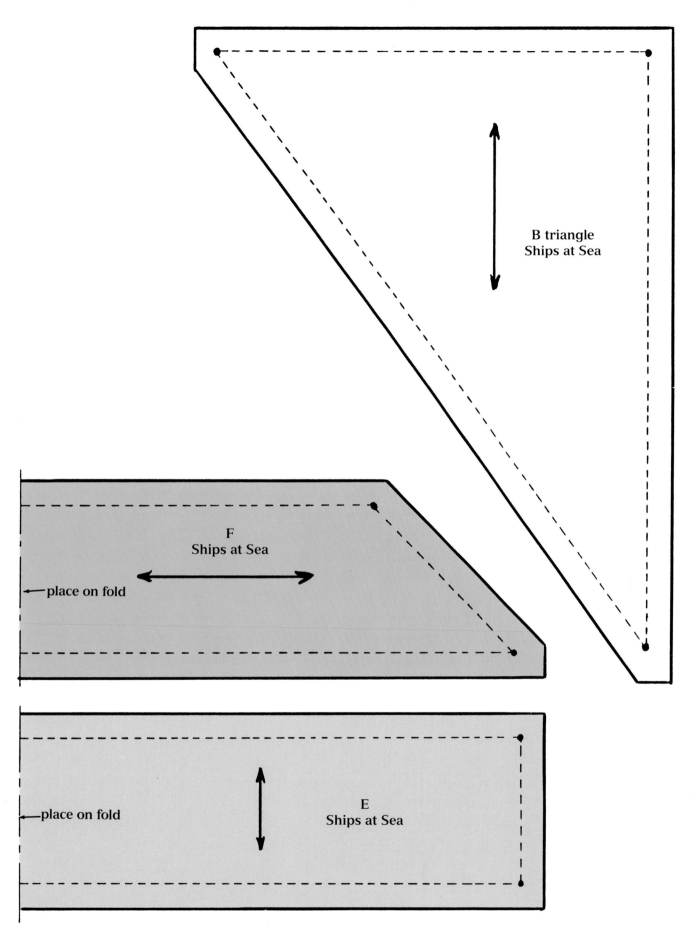

B triangle
Ships at Sea

F
Ships at Sea

← place on fold

E
Ships at Sea

← place on fold

Full-size patterns for quilt block, ctd.

Around-the-Square Lap Quilt

Materials Required

- *1 yard of a large-scale floral print fabric*

- *½ yard of rust mini-print or tone-on-tone fabric*

- *½ yard of green mini-print or tone-on-tone fabric*

- *½ yard EACH of two tan mini-print or solid fabrics*

- *44″ × 50″ piece of fabric of choice for the backing*

- *44″ × 50″ piece of quilt batting*

- *6 yards of ½″-wide bias binding (2″ wide when unfolded)*

- *Tan all-purpose thread and thread to match the bias binding*

This simple pattern works up very quickly. By adding extra yardage and extra blocks, you may make this quilt any size you wish. *Finished size of quilt: 41″ × 48″. Finished size of block: 7″ × 7″.*

Directions

The seam allowances are ¼″ throughout this quilt, and they are included in the patterns. Use the tan thread for the assembly. All piecing is done with right-sides of fabric facing.

1. From the large-scale floral print cut two strips, 3½″ × 42½″ each, for the A border strips and two strips, 3½″ × 41½″ each, for the B border strips. Set them aside.

2. From the remaining large-scale floral print cut 30 center squares using the square pattern. Using the strip pattern, cut 30 pieces of rust fabric, 30 pieces of green fabric, and 30 pieces from *each* of the tan fabrics.

3. Referring to Figure 6–1, stitch one rust strip to each center square, with the right sides facing; begin ¼″ in from the edge and sew up to but *not extending into* the converging seam allowance. Press the pieces open.

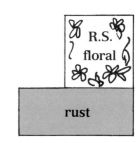

6–1. Stitch the rust strip to the center square. Don't sew into the side seam allowances of the square.

4. Now add one tan piece, starting at the edge of the rust strip and sewing across the floral center square (Fig. 6–2) to each unit made in Step 3. All the tan pieces joined should be of the same tan (tan 1). Press the unit open.

5. Add the green strip to the top of the unit for each unit (Fig. 6–3). Press the unit open.

6. Add the remaining tan strip (of the second tan) to the remaining side, stitching up to *but not onto* the rust strip. You will have a ¼" seam allowance hanging free where the short end of the tan strip meets the rust strip (Fig. 6–4a). Do not press yet.

7. Fold the block along the seamline of the rust strip and stitch the short seamline of the last tan strip to the remaining seamline of the rust strip (Fig. 6–4b). Now press the completed block. Repeat this for all 30 blocks.

8. Stitch 5 blocks together, with blocks oriented all in the same direction, to make one row (Fig. 6–5). Repeat for a total of 6 rows.

9. Stitch the 6 rows together to make the quilt center. Stitch the border strips cut in Step 1 to the quilt center as shown in Fig. 6–6; stitch the A strips to the sides and the B strips to the top and bottom.

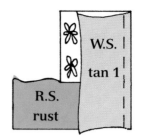
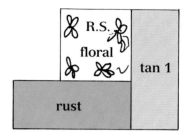

6–2. Stitch a tan strip of the first tan to the side of the center square.

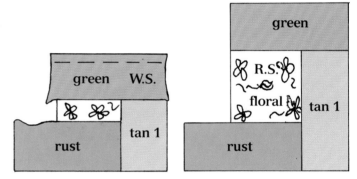

6–3. Stitch the green strip to the top of the unit.

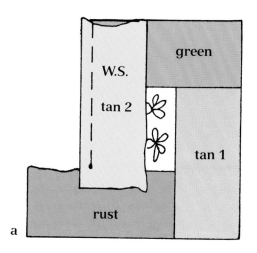
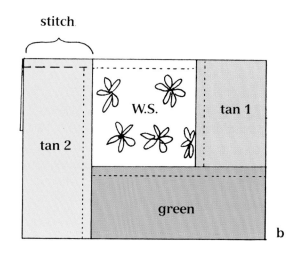
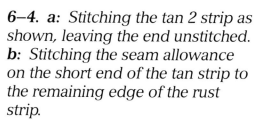

6–4. a: *Stitching the tan 2 strip as shown, leaving the end unstitched.* **b:** *Stitching the seam allowance on the short end of the tan strip to the remaining edge of the rust strip.*

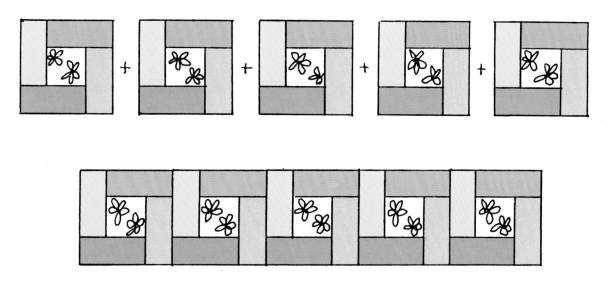

6–5. *Stitching 5 blocks together to make one row.*

10. Lay the backing fabric face down on your work surface and center the batting over the wrong side of the backing. Center the quilt top over the batting and thread-baste or pin-baste the layers together. Hand- or machine-quilt as desired. *

11. After quilting, baste around the raw edges of the quilt top, about ¼" in, and trim away the excess batting and backing. Bind the edges of the quilt with the bias binding, using thread to match the binding to complete this project.

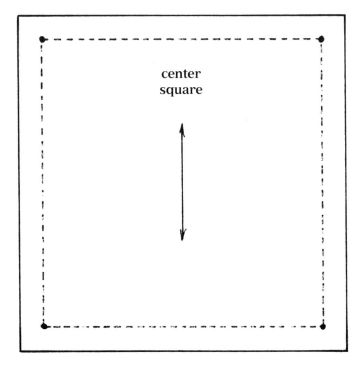

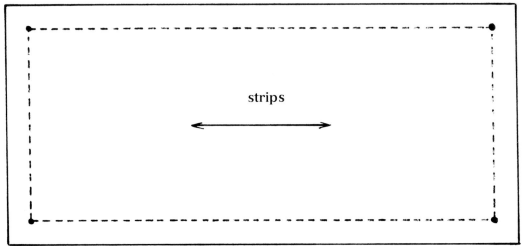

Full-size patterns for center square (3.5" × 3.5") and the strip (2½" × 5½"). Dashed line is stitching line.

*See the quilting pattern section at the back of the book for optional quilting patterns.

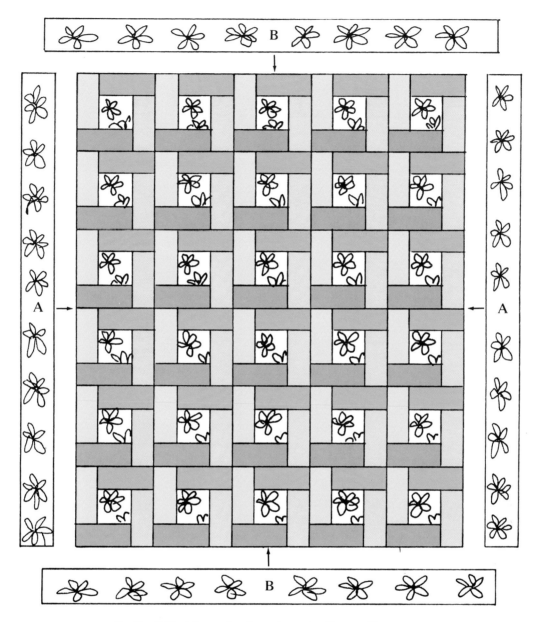

6–6. *Stitching the borders to the quilt center.*

Rows of Roses Wall Hanging and Pillow

Materials Required for Quilt and Pillow*

- *¾ yard light blue fabric*

- *½ yard green fabric*

- *½ yard deep red fabric*

- *⅓ yard EACH of 4 additional shades of pink or red*

- *35″ × 45″ piece of backing fabric*

- *35″ × 45″ piece of quilt batting*

- *15″ × 15″ piece of backing fabric for pillow*

- *15″ × 15″ piece of quilt batting for pillow*

- *4 yards of ½″-wide green satin ribbon*

- *14″ pillow form*

- *5 yards of ½″-wide bias binding (2″ wide when unfolded)*

- *All-purpose threads to match the fabrics*

*The pillow uses scraps from the quilt.

Feel free to substitute prints for the solid color fabrics in this project if you prefer. The flowers are assembled log-cabin style and are meant to be "scrappy": the pieces in the flowers should vary in their color arrangements. *Finished size of quilt: 33.5″ × 43.5″. Finished block size: 6″ × 6″. Finished size of the accent pillow: 14″ × 14″.*

Directions

Assembly is done with right sides of fabric facing. The seam allowances used are all ¼″ and are included in the given measurements.

For the Quilt
Refer to Fig. 7–1 for all quilt pieces.

1. From the green fabric cut 4 strips, each 2½″ × 26½″, for the A strips. Also from the green fabric, cut 2 strips, 2½″ × 35½″ each, for the B border strips. Set these strips aside.

2. From the deep red fabric cut 2 strips, 2½″ × 28½″ each, for the C strips, and cut 2 D strips 2½″ × 43½″ each; set these aside also.

3. From the shades of pink and red fabrics, including the deep red scraps, cut twenty-six 2½″ × 2½″ squares; these will be known as square #1. Set aside 8 of these squares to be used with the border strips. For nine of the remaining 18 #1 squares, cut a 2½″ × 4½″ piece of the same color fabric; for 9 use a contrasting color; these will be called piece #2. Cut 9 pieces, 2½″ × 6½″ each, one of each of the colors used for the contrasting #2 pieces; these are called piece #3.

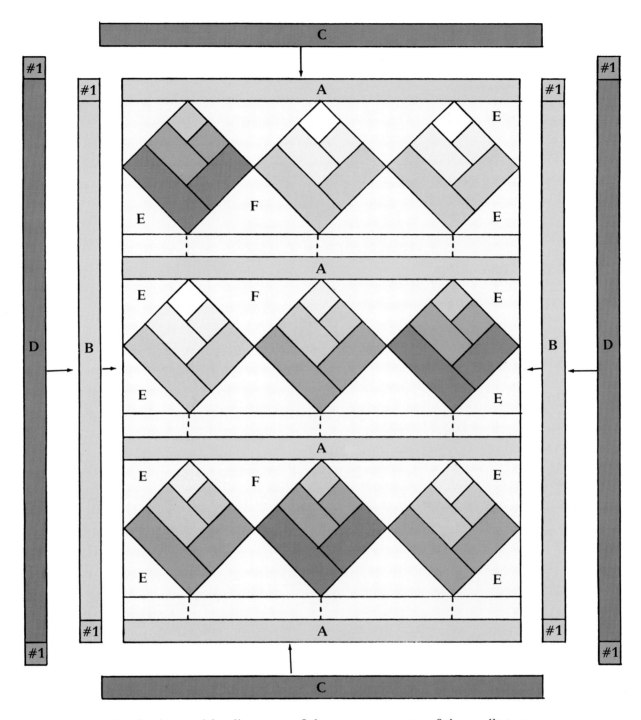

7–1. *Assembly diagram of the components of the quilt top.*

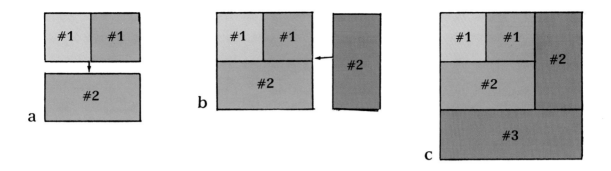

*7–2. Assembling the flower block in three stages, **a**, **b** and **c**.*

4. Referring to Figure 7–2, stitch together two #1 squares of two different pinks or reds; add on a #2 piece of the same color as the right #1 square (Figure 7-2a). Add on a second #2 piece of a contrasting red or pink (Fig. 7–2b). Last of all, add on a #3 piece the same color as the second #2 piece (Fig. 7–2c). Repeat to make a total of 9 pieced blocks, varying the color combinations you choose.

5. From the light blue fabric cut 3 7¼″ × 7¼″ squares. Cut each square into quarters on the diagonal to make a total of 12 E triangles (Fig. 7–3a). Also from the light blue fabric, cut 6 squares, each 6⅞″ × 6⅞″. Cut each of these squares in half on the diagonal to make a total of 12 F triangles (Fig. 7–3b).

6. Assemble 3 flower blocks along with 4 E triangles and 4 F triangles as shown in Figure 7–4, and stitch them together to make one flower row. Join the triangles to the blocks' edges first, as shown. Then sew the three units together (Fig. 7–4). Make 2 more rows

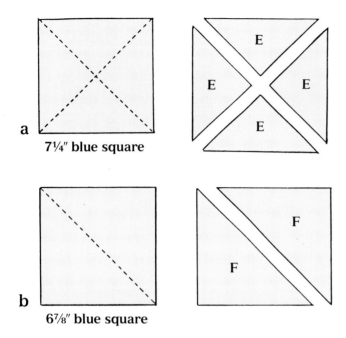

a

7¼″ blue square

b

6⅞″ blue square

*7–3. Cutting the blue squares into triangles. **a:** The quarter-square triangles (E). **b:** The half-square triangles (F).*

the same way. From the light blue fabric, cut 3 joiner strips 2½″ × 26½″ each, and stitch one strip to the bottom edge of each flower row (Fig. 7–5). Draw a line from the base of each flower and through the blue strip to mark the stem lines (see Fig. 7–1 for lines). Stitch a length of the green ribbon along each stem line. Sew an A strip to the top of each row of roses (see Fig. 7–1 for reference) and to the bottom of the lowest row also.

7. Take the B border strips and attach a #1 square to each short end. Do the same with the D border strips (see Fig. 7–1 for reference). Assemble the quilt by stitching together the 3 flower rows

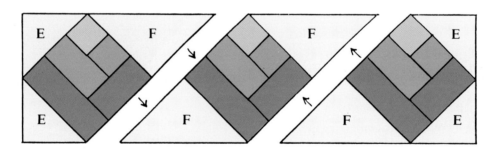

7–4. Assembling a flower row.

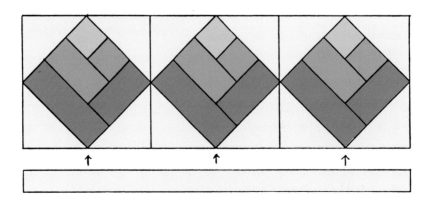

7–5. Stitching the light blue joiner strips to the bottoms of the flower rows.

and the border strips, as shown in the assembly diagram (Fig. 7–1).

8. Lay the backing fabric face down on your work surface, and center the batting over the backing. Center the quilt top over the batting and hand-baste or pin-baste the layers together. Machine-quilt the quilt as desired. After quilting, baste ¼″ in from the raw edges all around the quilt top, and trim away the excess batting and backing.

9. Divide the remaining ribbon into 10 pieces, reserving one piece for the pillow. Tie each length into a bow and tack it to the base of each flower to resemble leaves.

10. Bind the edges of the quilt with the bias binding.

For the Pillow
1. Make one flower block as you did for the quilt. Cut one light blue square that is 7¼″ × 7¼″; then cut it into quarters on the diagonals as for the quilt (Fig. 7–3a). Stitch one blue triangle to each side of the flower block. Press. From the green fabric cut 4 G strips, each 2½″ × 10½″. From the various shades of pink and red, cut 4 corner squares, 2½″ × 2½″ each. Stitch one square to each short end of two of the green G strips. Stitch

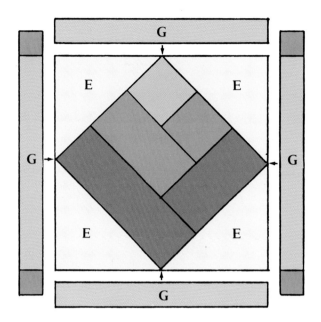

7–6. Assembling the pillow top.

the strips to the pillow top as shown in Figure 7–6.

2. Baste the square of batting to the wrong side of the pillow top and quilt as desired. Then place the pillow top and the backing fabric together, with right sides facing, and stitch along the sides, leaving a 10″ opening along the bottom edge for turning it right-side out. Clip the corners of the seam allowances and turn the pillow cover right-side out. Insert the pillow form and hand-stitch the opening closed. Tie the reserved length of ribbon into a bow and tack it to the base of the flower block.

Confetti Four-Patch Lap Quilt

Materials Required

· *2 yards of light brown print fabric (small allover print) or solid light brown*

· *1 yard medium-green print fabric for the borders*

· *2¼ yards TOTAL of scrap yardage in many colors (Tip: If you don't have enough scraps in your basket, head to the fabric store and purchase eight ¼-yard cuts in the fabrics of your choice)*

· *All-purpose threads to match fabrics*

· *47″ × 59″ piece of quilt batting*

· *47″ × 59″ piece of backing fabric of choice*

· *5 yards of ½″-wide bias binding (2″ wide when unfolded)*

This is a scrap-basket quilt; you can use up all of your fabric odds and ends when you make it. This will give you an excuse to make a trip to the fabric store to replenish your supply! *Finished size of quilt: 46″ × 58″. Finished block size: 4″ × 4″ (without seam allowances).*

Directions

The quilt center is made of 63 pieced blocks, set on point, alternating with 48 solid blocks, with solid triangles set around. Construction is done with ¼″ seam allowances and right sides of fabric facing throughout. The seam allowances are included in the patterns and in all of the given measurements.

1. From the scrap yardage cut a total of 252 A squares, each 2½″ × 2½″. Stitch 4 A squares together randomly to make a 4-patch block (Fig. 8–1).

2. From the light brown fabric cut 48 B squares, each 4½″ × 4½″, for the setting squares. Also from the light brown fabric cut 28 C triangles for setting around the edges and 4 D triangles for the corners of the quilt center.

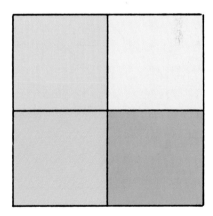

8–1. The completed 4-patch block. Make 63 of these.

3. Referring to the row diagram (Fig. 8–2), assemble rows 1 through 15. The rows are shown and numbered diagonally, as

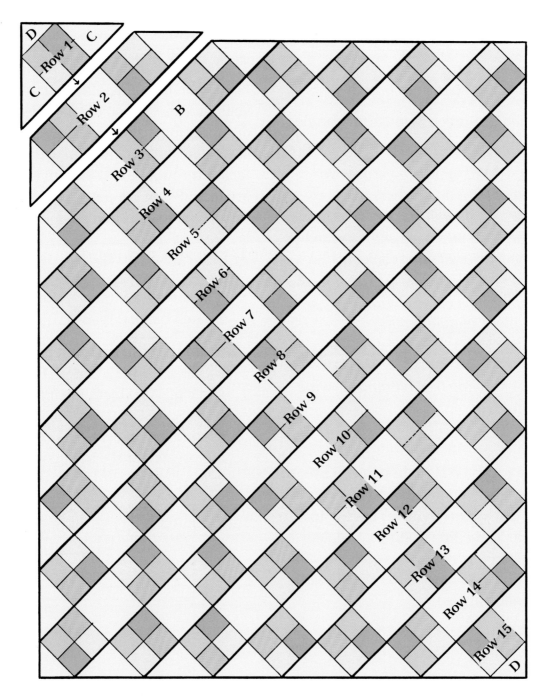

8–2. *The row construction diagram for quilt center.*

this is the way in which the quilt center is constructed. It's very easy! To avoid making the same row twice, check off the rows you have already completed, and tag them with a piece of masking tape to make assembly easier.

4. From the green print fabric, cut two E side border strips, each 3½″ wide, and as long as the side of your quilt center, and stitch one to each side of the quilt center (Fig. 8–3). From the same fabric, cut two F strips that are 3½″ wide and equal to the width of the quilt center across the top plus the side borders' widths (see Fig. 8–3). Sew them to the top and bottom of the quilt center.

5. Lay the backing fabric face down on your work surface. Center the batting over the wrong side of the backing and center the quilt top over the batting. Hand-baste or pin-baste the layers together and hand- or machine-quilt as desired. Then baste all around the quilt top, ¼″ in from the raw edges of the quilt top.

6. Trim away the excess batting and backing fabric and bind the quilt with the bias binding to complete it.

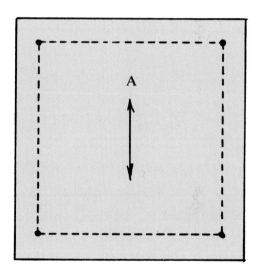

Template for the A square (2½″ × 2½″).

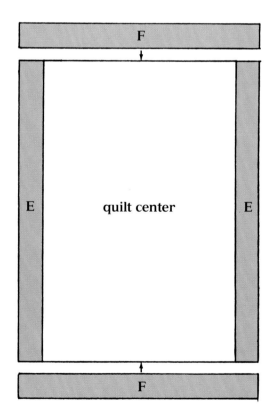

8–3. *Stitching the borders to the quilt center.*

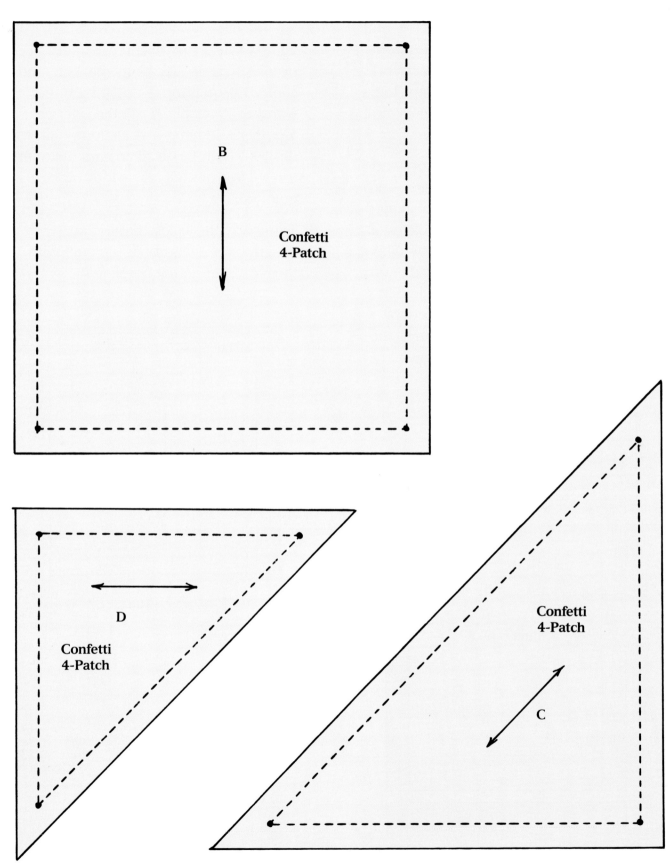

Templates for the B square (4½″ × 4½″) and C and D triangles.

Birthday Banner

Materials Required*

· *13½" × 15½" piece of white print fabric*

· *¼ yard pink print fabric*

· *¼ yard blue print fabric*

· *⅛ yard green print fabric*

· *Scraps of yellow fabric*

· *Scrap of light orange solid fabric (for flames)*

· *1 yard of fusible webbing (14" wide)*

· *21" × 23" piece of backing fabric of choice*

· *21" × 23" piece of low-loft batting or fleece*

· *2½ yards ½"-wide yellow bias binding (2" wide when unfolded)*

· *Black fine-point permanent marker*

· *All-purpose sewing thread in a neutral color*

*Use small overall print designs or solid colors.

This project uses a simple no-sew technique to give the look of quilting. Instead of stitching by hand or machine, the black quilting lines are actually drawn on the fabric using a fine-point permanent marker. Some sewing is still required for the assembly of this project. *Finished size of banner: 19" × 21"*

Directions

1. Trace the appliqué pieces (cake, candles, candle holders, flames, frosting, drip, and plate) onto the paper side of fusible webbing. As for the candles, I have used 5 in the sample, but you may use as many as you like. Cut them all out of the webbing.

2. From the pink print fabric, cut four strips, each 1½" × 15½", for the A and B border strips (see Fig. 9–1). Set them aside. Fuse the webbing frosting and

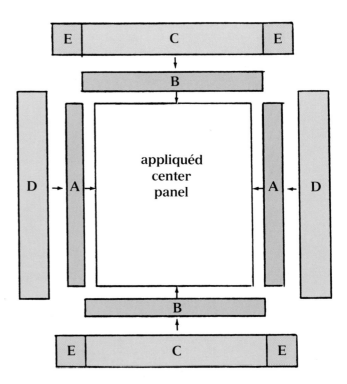

9–1. *Attaching the border strips and the green corner units.*

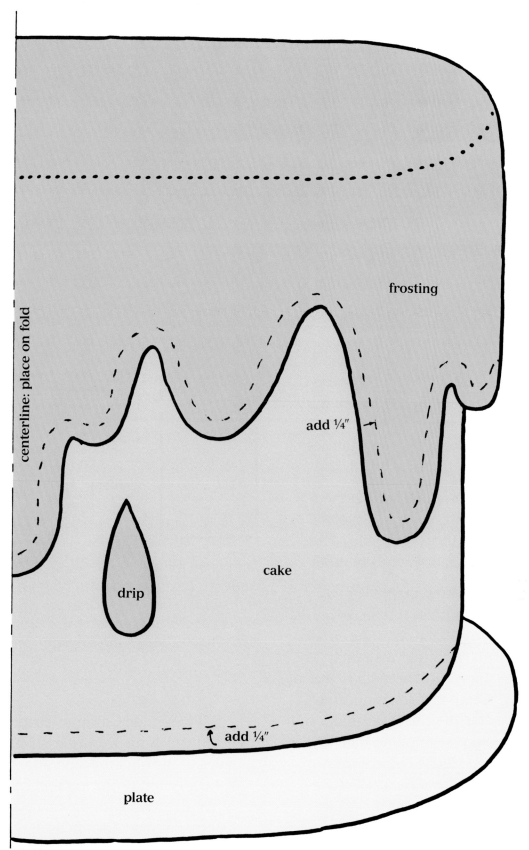

frosting

centerline: place on fold

add ¼"

cake

drip

add ¼"

plate

Half templates for the cake, frosting, drip, and plate. Trace out the templates, adding ¼" above the wavy line of the cake and above the top of the plate, so the appliqués' edges can overlap where they meet when you fuse them. Cut out all pieces on folded webbing. Seam allowances aren't included or needed for machine appliqué. Add ¼" seam allowances for hand appliqué.

drip to the wrong side of the remaining pink fabric, and cut them out of the fabric. Set them aside.

3. From the blue print fabric, cut 2 C border strips, each 2½″ × 15½″, and two D border strips, each 2½″ × 17½″, and set them aside. Fuse the webbing candles cut in Step 1 to the wrong side of the remaining blue print fabric, and cut them out of the fabric.

4. Fuse the webbing plate and the webbing candle holders, cut in Step 1, to the wrong side of the yellow scrap fabric. Fuse the flames to the wrong side of the light orange scrap fabric. Cut out all the shapes from the fabrics.

5. From the green fabric, cut 4 E squares, each 2½″ × 2½″, and set them aside with the border strips. Fuse the webbing cake to the wrong side of the remaining green fabric, and cut it out.

6. Fold the white print rectangle in half on its length, and press it to make a center line. Fuse all the cake pieces to the white print rectangle, aligning center lines. First fuse the plate to the white print, about 1½ inches up from the bottom; fuse the cake over that; fuse the frosting overlapping that; fuse the candles and candle holders over that. Fuse the drip and flames last. Be sure the pieces are securely fused, as you will not be stitching these pieces to the base fabric.

7. Stitch the A and B border pieces to the center unit as shown in Figure 9–1. Take the green E squares cut in Step 5, and attach one to each short end of a

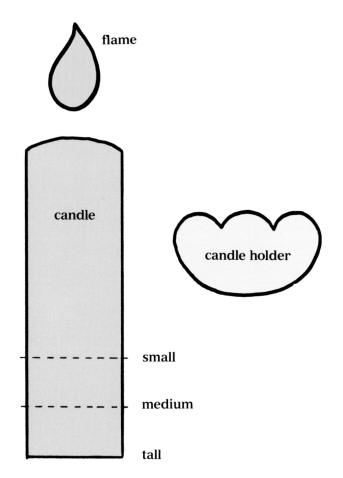

Templates for the candle, candle holder, and flame. Cut as many as you want of each out of fusible webbing. You can vary the length of the candles if you like. (Add ¼″ seam allowances if you hand appliqué.)

2½″ × 15½″ blue C border strip (see Fig. 9–1). Attach the D border strips to the sides of the quilt top, and attach the E + C + E unit to the top and bottom. Stitch them on with the neutral thread, using ¼″ seam allowances.

8. Lay the backing fabric face down on your work surface, and center the quilt batting over the wrong side of the backing fabric. Center the quilt top face up over the batting and pin-baste

Closeup showing pen stitch.

the layers together. Machine quilt along the seamlines of the borders to secure the layers. Then baste around the quilt top, ¼″ in from the raw edges, and trim away the excess batting and backing fabric.

9. Bind the quilt with the bias binding, using all-purpose thread to match the binding fabric.

10. Using the permanent pen, make stitch marks around the appliqué pieces, approximately ¼″ from the edges of the appliqués (see Fig. 9–2 and photos). Also make stitch marks

through the center of the pink border strips and in the green corner squares.

11. Enjoy! Wasn't that quick and simple?

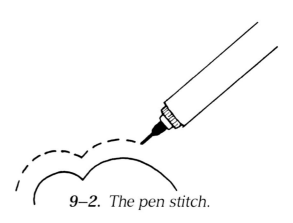

9–2. The pen stitch.

Watering Can Wall Hanging

Materials Required*

· *½ yard tan print fabric*

· *⅓ yard EACH light blue and medium blue print fabrics*

· *⅛ yard dark blue print fabric*

· *⅓ yard dark rose print fabric*

· *1 yard fusible webbing (18″ width) or equivalent*

· *3½ yards of ½″-wide bias binding (2″ wide when unfolded)*

· *22″ × 36″ piece of low-loft batting*

· *22″ × 36″ piece of backing fabric of choice*

· *Threads to match all of the fabrics*

*Use small overall prints for all the print fabrics.

Perky watering cans and hearts make for a cute little quilt for "that spot" on the wall. *Finished size of wall hanging: 20″ × 34″. Block size: 12″ × 12″.*

Directions

All piecing is done with ¼″ seam allowances and right sides of fabric facing. Appliqué patterns are given without seam allowances, as they aren't needed for machine appliqué; add ¼″ seam allowances around all appliqué patterns if you will do hand appliqué.

1. Trace one complete watering can, including the spout and handle, and one complete reversed watering can onto the paper side of fusible webbing. Cut out the cans and fuse one webbing can to the wrong side of the light blue fabric and one to the wrong side of the medium blue fabric, and cut out the cans, spouts, and handles.

2. Trace and cut out 2 sets of webbing can openings and bands around the can and spout onto the paper side of the webbing; one set should have reversed patterns. Cut out the webbing pieces. Fuse the webbing can openings and spout openings to the wrong side of the dark blue fabric and cut them out.

3. Fuse one set of webbing bands (around the can and the spout) to the wrong side of the light blue print fabric and one set to the wrong side of the medium blue fabric, and cut them out. Fuse the light blue bands to the medium blue can and the medium blue bands to the light blue can.

4. Trace 6 hearts onto the paper side of the remaining webbing, and cut them out. Cut out and fuse 2 to the wrong sides of each of the following fabrics: the dark rose fabric, the light blue fabric, and the medium blue fabric. Cut out all the hearts from the fabrics. Fuse one dark rose heart to the center of each of the watering cans (see Fig. 10–1). Set the other hearts aside for now.

5. From the tan fabric cut 2 squares, each 12½″ × 12½″. Press each in half vertically to mark the center line. Fuse one complete watering can, centered, on each square. Machine-appliqué all the pieces in place, using matching

Closeup showing machine appliqué.

10–1. *A complete watering can. The second can reverses the light and medium blue fabrics.*

threads, with a medium-width machine satin stitch.

6. From the light blue fabric, cut two A strips, 1½″ × 12½″ each, and two B strips, 1½″ × 14½″ each. Stitch the two A strips to the side of the block with the medium blue can (Fig. 10–2). Stitch the two B strips to the remaining 2 sides of the same block. Cut 2 A and 2 B strips from the medium-blue fabric and stitch them to the block with the light blue can. Press.

7. Stitch the 2 blocks together as shown in Figure 10–3.

8. From the deep rose fabric cut 2 side border C strips, 3½″ × 28½″ each, and stitch them to the sides of the 2-block unit (Fig. 10–3). Press. Cut two D strips, 3½″ × 20½″ each, and stitch them to the top and bottom. Press.

10–2. Attaching A and B borders.

9. Fuse one blue heart to each corner of the quilt top at the corners of the blue strips (see photo). Machine-appliqué the hearts in place with blue thread and a medium-width satin stitch (Fig. 10–4).

10. Lay the backing fabric face down on your work surface. Center the quilt batting over the backing fabric and center the quilt top, face up, over the batting. Pin-baste the layers together.

11. Hand- or machine-quilt the wall hanging as desired. Then baste all around the edges of the quilt top, ¼″ in from the edge, and trim away the excess batting and backing fabric.

12. Bind the edges of the quilt with the bias binding to complete it.

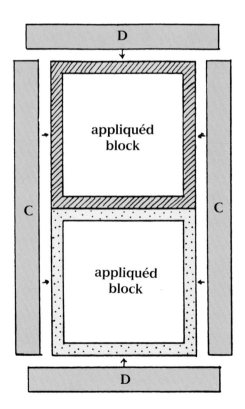

10–3. Stitch the 2 blocks together vertically. Then add the C and D borders.

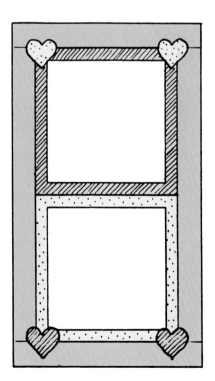

10–4. Fuse the hearts to the corners of the quilt top.

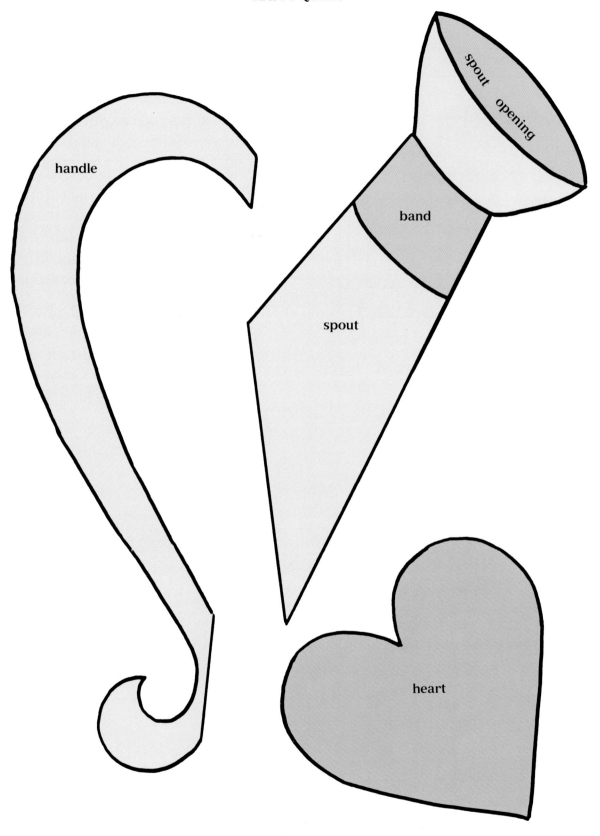

Full-size appliqué patterns of handle, spout, band, spout opening, and heart. Seam allowances aren't included (not needed for machine appliqué). Add ¼″ seam allowance for hand appliqué.

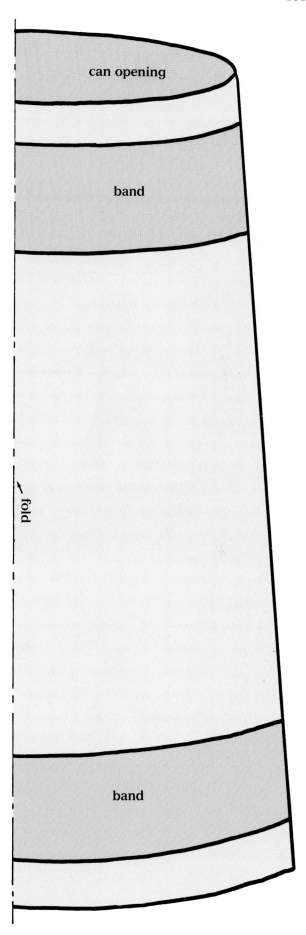

Full-size appliqué pattern for the watering can, bands, and can opening. Cut on folded webbing. Add ¼" seam allowances if you plan to do hand appliqué.

Paper Dolls Wall Hanging

Materials Required

· ¾ yard ecru fabric

· ⅓ yard bright green print for sashing

· ½ yard multicolored print fabric

· ⅓ yard EACH: yellow, blue, and orange fabrics

· 1½ yards fusible webbing (14″ wide)

· 35″ × 36″ piece of low-loft quilt batting or fleece

· 35″ × 36″ piece of backing fabric of choice

· 4 yards of ½″-wide bias binding (2″ wide when unfolded)

· Threads to match the fabrics

This quilt can be personalized as you see fit. Use all girls, all boys, or a combination; use fewer blocks or add more, adjusting the size of the borders as needed. *Finished size of quilt: 33″ × 34″. Block size: 9 × 12″* (without seam allowances).

Directions

Appliqué patterns don't include seam allowances, as they are not needed for machine appliqué. Add ¼″ seam allowances if you will do hand appliqué. Construction is done with ¼″ seam allowances.

1. From the ecru fabric cut 6 blocks, each 9½″ × 12½″, and press them in half lengthwise to make a centerline. Set them aside.

2. Trace a total of 6 dolls (of the genders of your choice) and 6 hearts onto the paper side of fusible interfacing, and cut them out.

3. Fuse two of the webbing dolls to the wrong side of each of the following fabrics: yellow, blue, and orange. Fuse the hearts to the wrong side of the green fabric. Cut out all of the appliqués. Fuse one heart to each of the dolls (see photo for position).

4. Fuse one doll to the right side of each of the ecru blocks, centered on the centerline. Machine-appliqué all the pieces in place on the blocks, using matching threads and a medium-width satin stitch.

5. Lay out all six blocks in two rows of three. Stitch 3 blocks in the first row together along their long sides. Repeat with the remaining three blocks to make a second row (Fig. 11–1).

11–1. *A completed 3-block row.*

6. From the green print fabric cut 4 A strips, 1½″ × 27½″ each. Stitch one A strip to each long side of the 3-block strips (Fig. 11–2).

7. Also from the green print fabric cut 4 B strips, 1½″ × 14½″ each, and stitch one to each short side of the 3-block row (Fig 11–2).

8. From the multicolored print, cut 3 C strips, 2½″ × 29½″ each. Stitch them above, between, and below the two 3-block rows, as shown in Figure 11–3.

9. Also from the multicolored print, cut two D strips, 2½″ × 34½″ each. Stitch them to the sides of the quilt center as shown in Figure 11–3. Press.

10. Lay the backing fabric face down and center the batting over the backing. Center the quilt top over the batting. Hand-baste or pin-baste the layers together and hand- or machine-quilt as desired.

11. Baste about ¼″ in from the raw edges all around the quilt top, and trim away the excess batting and backing. Bind the edges of the quilt with the bias binding.

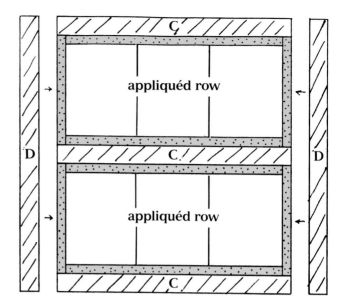

11–3. Stitching the multicolored C and D strips to the three-block rows as sashing and borders.

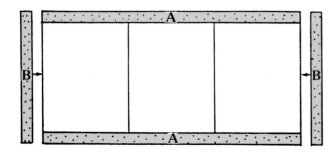

11–2. Stitch the green A and B strips to the three-block rows.

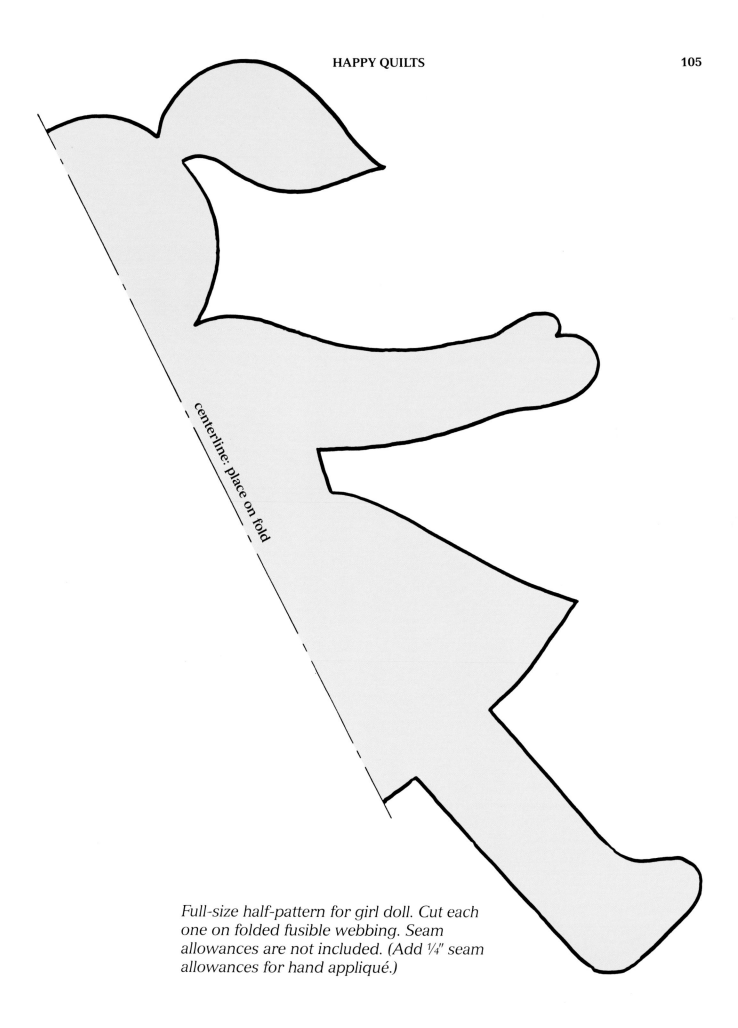

centerline: place on fold

Full-size half-pattern for girl doll. Cut each one on folded fusible webbing. Seam allowances are not included. (Add ¼″ seam allowances for hand appliqué.)

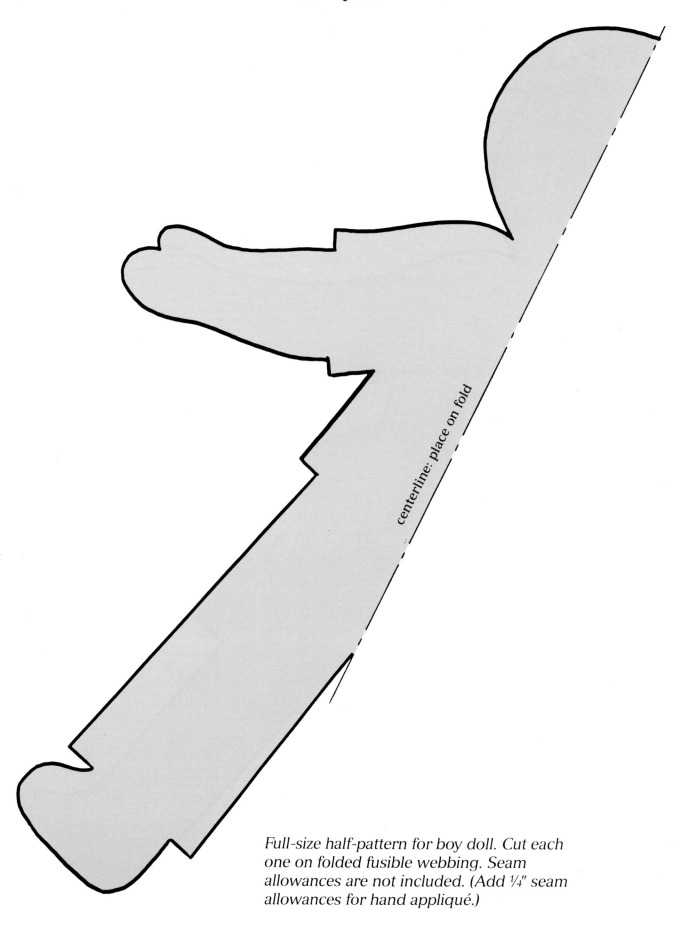

centerline: place on fold

Full-size half-pattern for boy doll. Cut each one on folded fusible webbing. Seam allowances are not included. (Add ¼" seam allowances for hand appliqué.)

Stepped Star Quilt

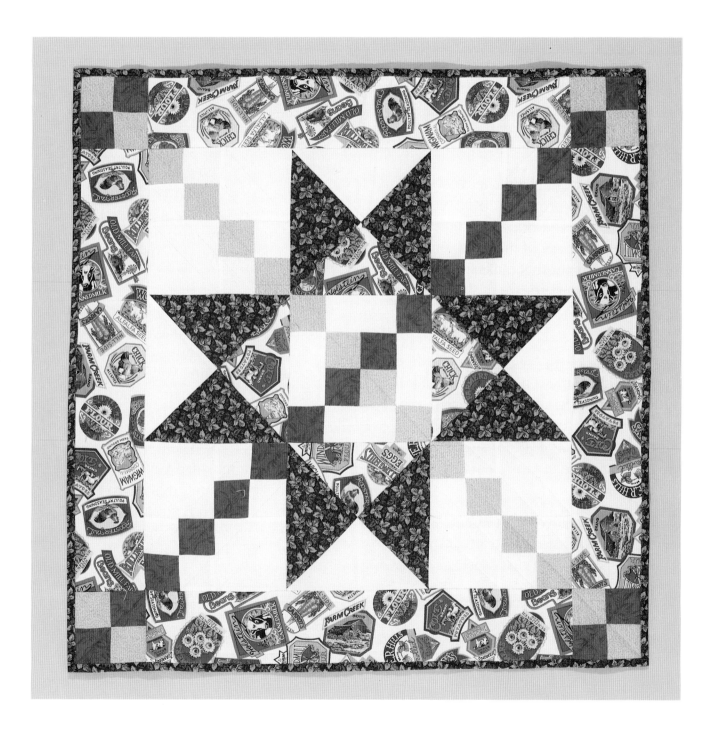

Materials Required

- *½ yard novelty-print fabric with a large-scale design*

- *½ yard off-white solid fabric*

- *⅓ yard EACH green, mustard yellow, and rust fabrics*

- *34" × 34" piece of quilt batting*

- *34" × 34" piece of backing fabric of choice*

- *Neutral-colored thread for assembly*

Have you ever admired those wonderful "novelty" cotton prints in the fabric stores, but been unable to find a way to use them? This quilt takes care of that problem. It's the "novelty" print that makes this easy quilt special. *Finished size of the quilt: 32" × 32".*

Directions

The seam allowances are all ¼" and are included in all of the given measurements and pattern pieces. All construction is done with right sides of fabric facing.

1. From the green fabric cut 8 A triangles.

2. From the yellow fabric cut 20 small (2½" × 2½") B squares. Cut 20 small B squares from the rust fabric as well.

3. From the off-white fabric, cut 8 large C squares (4½" × 4½"). Cut 16 B squares, 4 D rectangles (2½" × 4½") and 4 A triangles from the off-white fabric also.

4. From the novelty-print fabric cut 4 A triangles and 4 I border strips, each 4½" × 24½".

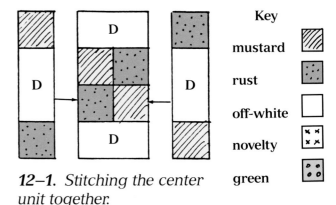

12–1. *Stitching the center unit together.*

Key:
- mustard
- rust
- off-white
- novelty
- green

5. To make the center unit, first make a 4-patch of 2 yellow and 2 rust B squares. Attach an off-white D rectangle above and below the 4-patch, as shown in the center of Figure 12–1.

6. Piece a side unit from a yellow and a rust B square, each attached to a short side of a D rectangle. Piece another side unit the same way, and sew one side unit to each side of the 4-patch unit made in Step 5 (see Fig. 12–1). Set the center unit aside.

7. To make a mustard yellow and off-white corner unit, make two 4 patches from 4 mustard B squares and 4 off-white B squares, as shown in Figure 12–2a. Then take two off-white C squares and attach a C square to each 4-patch, as shown in Figure 12–2a. Then join the 2 units to make a double 4-patch, as shown in Figure 12–2b. Make another corner unit of mustard and off-white in the same way.

8. To make the two rust and off-white corner units, repeat Step 7, using 4 rust B squares and 4 off-white B

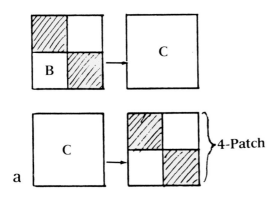

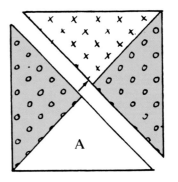

12–3. *Make a 4-triangle square, as shown.*

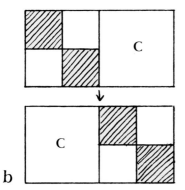

12–2. *Stitching a corner unit.* **a:** *Join the 4-patches to the C blocks.* **b.** *Join the C block + 4-patch to another C block + 4-patch.*

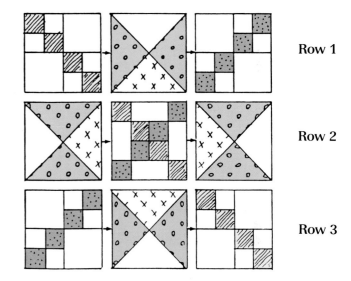

12–4. *Stitch all of the units into 3 rows; then join the rows to make the completed quilt center.*

squares, and 2 off-white C squares for each corner unit.

9. Take two green A triangles, along with one off-white A triangle and one novelty print A triangle; sew them together to make one complete 4-triangle square, as shown in Figure 12–3. Make 3 more 4-triangle squares the same way. Press them.

10. Lay out the units as shown in Fig. 12–4 on your work surface. Stitch all of the units together to make the quilt center: make 3 rows of 3 pieced blocks first; then sew the rows together.

11. Using the remaining rust B squares and yellow B squares, make four 4-patch border corners, as shown in Figure 12–5, and stitch one to each short end of a novelty print I border strip. positioned as shown in Figure 12–5, to make a border unit.

12. Stitch the remaining I strips to the top and bottom of the quilt center. Then stitch the I border units from Step 11

12–5. *Make two border units of 4-patch +
I strip + 4-patch.*

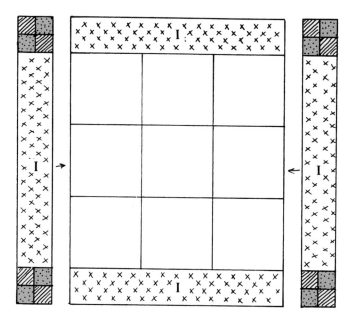

to the remaining two sides of the quilt
center (Fig. 12–6). This completes the
quilt top.

13. Lay the backing fabric face down on
your work surface and center the quilt
batting over the wrong side of the
backing fabric. Center the quilt top,
face up, over the batting, and hand-
baste or pin-baste the layers together.
Hand- or machine-quilt, as desired.
Baste around the raw edges of the
quilt top, ¼″ in from the raw edge, and
trim away the excess batting and
backing. Bind the edges of the quilt
with the bias binding.

12–6. *Stitch an I border to the top and to the
bottom of the quilt center. Then stitch the 2
border units to the sides.*

Closeup of quilt center, showing machine quilting.

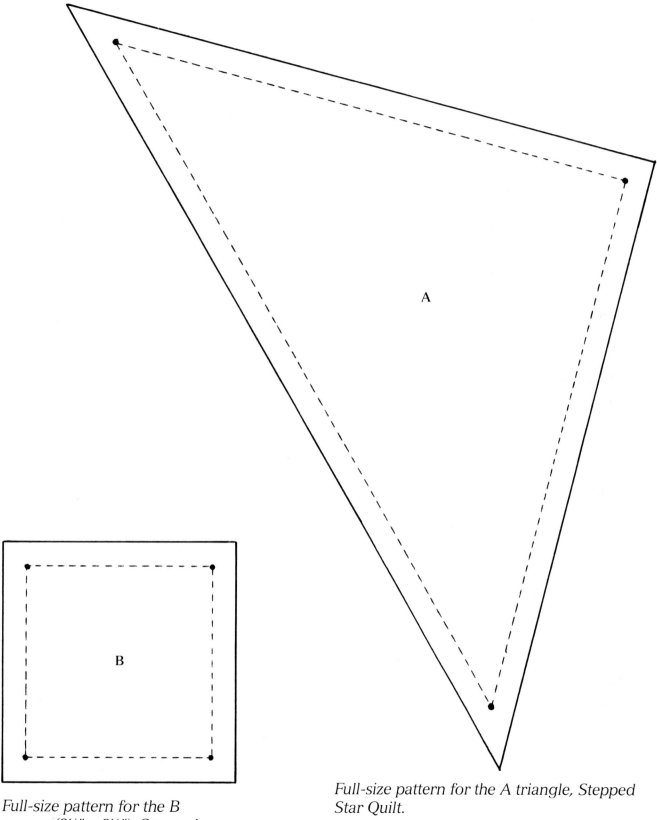

A

B

Full-size pattern for the B square (2½″ × 2½″), Stepped Star Quilt.

Full-size pattern for the A triangle, Stepped Star Quilt.

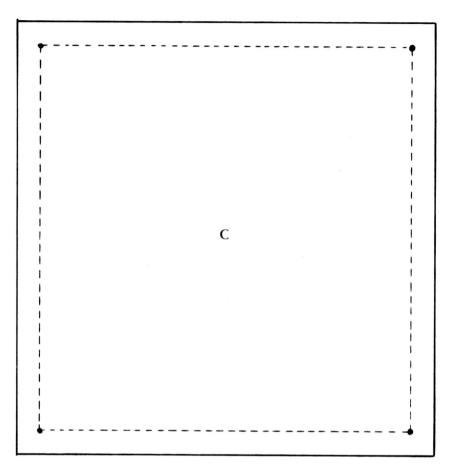

Full-size pattern for C square (4½″ × 4½″), Stepped Star Quilt.

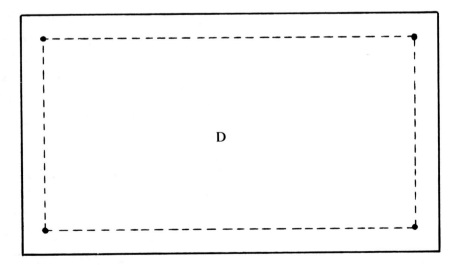

Full-size pattern for the D rectangle (2½″ × 4½″), Stepped Star Quilt.

Birdies' Little Abode Wall Hanging and Pillow

Materials Required

For the Quilt
- *14½″ × 19½″ piece of off-white print or off-white fabric (small allover print)*
- *¼ yard pink print fabric for the inner border*
- *⅓ yard blue print for the outer border*
- *1 yard of fusible webbing (18″ width) or equivalent*
- *Scraps of light yellow and medium yellow fabric for the birds*
- *Scraps of various pastel fabrics, plus scraps of brown, tan print, and ecru for the birdhouses*
- *Scraps of dark green fabrics for the leaves*
- *28″ × 23″ piece of low-loft batting*
- *28″ × 23″ piece of backing fabric of choice*
- *3½ yards of ½″ wide bias binding (2″ wide when unfolded)*
- *Threads to match all of the fabrics used*

"Cheep" housing for the birds—but no cats allowed! Use fabric scraps to make this little number. *Finished size of wall hanging: 25″ × 20″. Finished size of pillow: 12″ × 12″.*

Directions

Seam allowances aren't included or needed for machine appliqué. Add ¼″ seam allowances around all appliqué pieces if you will do hand appliqué. Assembly of borders is done with ¼″ seam allowances and right sides of fabric facing.

For the Pillow
- *6½″ × 6½″ piece of off-white solid or off-white print fabric*
- *Scraps of the pink and blue fabrics listed above*
- *12½″ × 12½″ piece of low-loft batting*
- *12½″ × 12½″ piece of backing fabric of choice*
- *12″ polyester pillow form*
- *Scraps of pastel fabrics and yellows, as listed above*
- *¼ yard fusible webbing (18″ width) or equivalent*
- *2 yards of off-white piping*
- *Threads to match all fabrics*

For the Quilt
1. Trace out the two parts of the large birdhouse pattern and join them with tape. Trace one of each size of birdhouse (small, medium, and large) onto the paper side of fusible webbing. Also on the paper side of the webbing, trace: one sitting bird and one reversed sitting bird, one flying bird and one reversed flying bird, and one reversed bird head in the circle. Cut out and fuse the webbing bodies of the birds to the wrong side of the light yellow fabric and fuse the webbing wings to the wrong side of the medium yellow fabric. Fuse the houses, roofs, and birdhouse holes to the various fabric

scraps on the wrong sides (see photo). Fuse a 3″ × 5″ piece of fusible webbing to a like-size piece of tan scrap yardage. Cut three ½″ × 3″ strips from this tan piece for the poles. Cut one shorter for the large birdhouse.

2. Referring to the color photo, fuse the 3 poles and the 3 birdhouses to the piece of off-white fabric. Fuse the roofs and holes on also. Fuse the birds on where you wish, fusing the bird head in the circle to one of the birdhouse holes.

3. Trace the 2 sets of reversed leaves onto the paper side of the remaining fusible webbing, cut them out, and fuse each set to the wrong side of a different green fabric. Cut out the leaves and fuse one set to each of the 2 smaller

birdhouses in the pole area (see photos).

4. Machine appliqué all of the pieces in place, using threads that match the fabrics and a medium-width satin stitch. Using a narrow machine satin stitch and green thread, stitch some vines to the two sets of leaves.

5. If you wish to make a sign for the birdhouse, cut a 1″ × 1½″ piece of fusible webbing and fuse it to the wrong side of a scrap of ecru fabric. Cut out the rectangle and fuse it to one of the bird-houses. Using a waterproof marking pen, write *FOR RENT—No Cats!* on the little rectangle. Appliqué the rectangle in place with matching thread.

6. From the pink fabric, cut two inner border A strips, 1½″ × 19½″ each, and stitch them to the longer sides of the appliquéd rectangle. Cut two B strips, 1½″ × 16½″ each, from the same fabric and stitch them to the remaining 2 sides (see Fig. 13–1). Press.

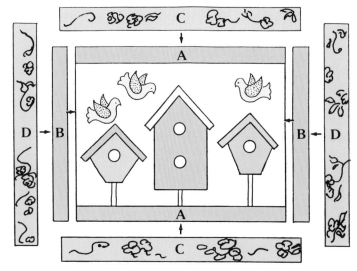

13–1. Stitching the borders to the quilt center.

7. From the blue fabric, cut two outer border C strips, 2½" × 22" each. Stitch them to the long sides of the quilt center. Cut two D strips 2½" × 20½" each, and stitch them to the remaining 2 sides (see Fig. 13–1). Press.

8. Lay the backing fabric face down and center the quilt batting over the backing fabric; center the quilt top, face up, over the batting. Hand-baste or pin-baste the layers together, and machine quilt as desired. Then baste around the raw edges of the quilt top, ¼" in from the edges, all around, and trim away the excess batting and backing. Bind the quilt with the bias binding to complete the quilt.

For the Pillow

1. Trace and fuse one birdhouse, and one roof, pole, and birdhouse hole, plus one reversed sitting bird, onto the paper side of fusible webbing. Cut out the webbing pieces, and fuse each to the wrong side of the correct fabric (see photo); cut out the appliqués. Then fuse the birdhouse and bird plus other parts, centered, on the 6½" off-white square. Machine appliqué the pieces in place with matching threads.

2. From the pink inner border fabric, cut two E strips, 1½" × 6½" each, and two F strips, 1½" × 8½" each. From the blue fabric cut two G strips, 2½" × 8½" each, and two H strips 2½" × 12½" each. Stitch the strips to the pillow center as shown in Figure 13–2.

3. Back the pillow top with the square of batting and machine quilt it if you wish.

4. Baste the piping around the edges of the pillow top, having the raw edges of the piping even with the raw edges of the quilt top.

5. Stitch the pillow top to the backing fabric, with right sides of fabric facing, along 3 sides. Clip the corners of the seam allowances, and turn the pillow cover right-side out. Insert the pillow form and hand-stitch the opening closed.

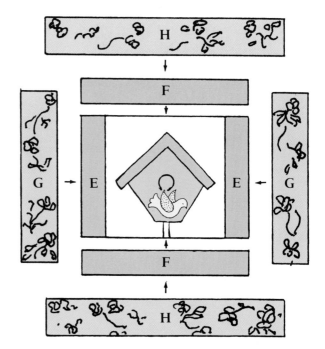

13–2. Stitching the borders to the pillow-top center.

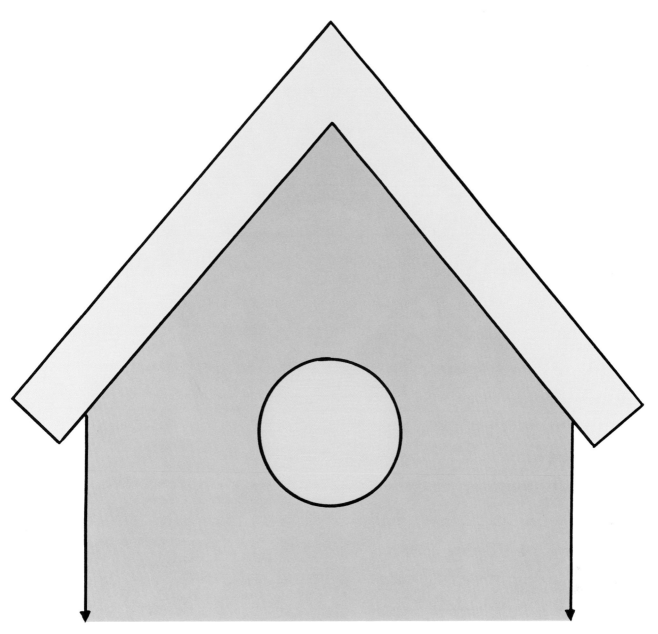

Upper portion of large birdhouse pattern (full size). Attach to lower portion of pattern at arrows before cutting out of fabric.

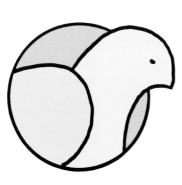

Bird's head in circle pattern (full size).

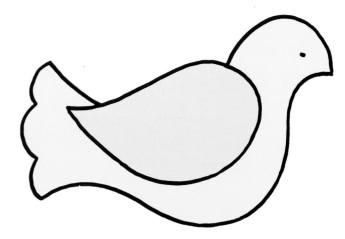

Sitting bird pattern (full size).

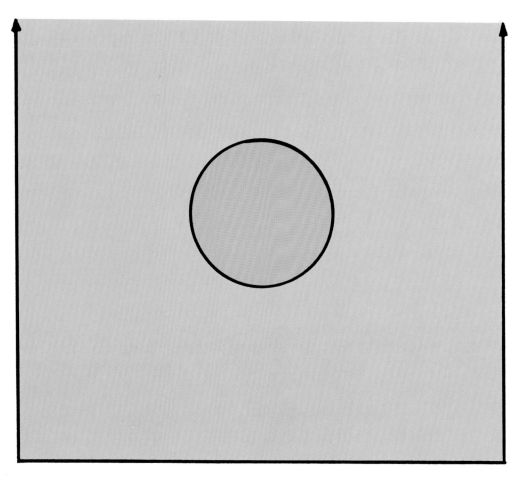

Lower portion of large birdhouse pattern (full size).

Flying bird pattern (full size).

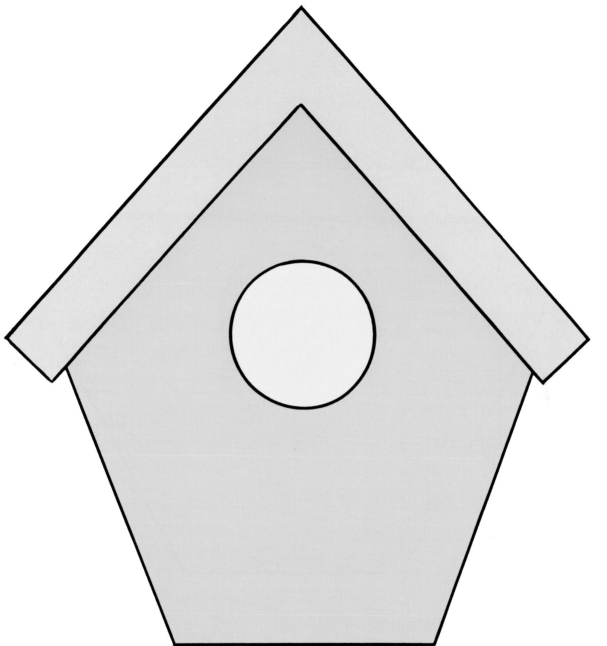

Medium-sized birdhouse pattern (full size).

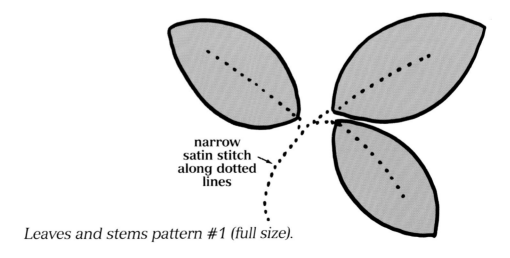

**narrow
satin stitch
along dotted
lines**

Leaves and stems pattern #1 (full size).

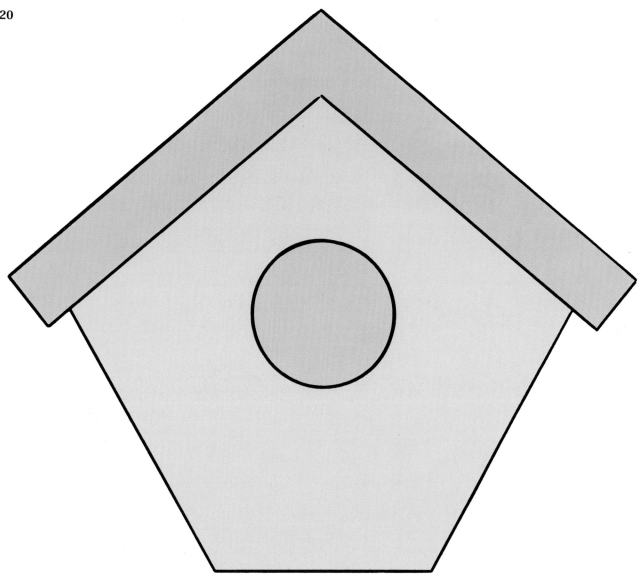

Small birdhouse pattern (full size).

FOR RENT
No
Cats!

Pattern for birdhouse sign.

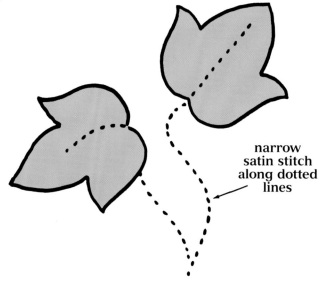

narrow
satin stitch
along dotted
lines

Leaves and stems pattern #2 (full size).

Wind Song Lap Quilt and Runner Set

Materials Required

For the Runner

· *Two 14½" × 6½" strips of off-white fabric*

· *Three 6" × 8" pieces of fabric: one each rust, yellow, and green prints for the leaves*

· *14½" × 22½" piece of multicolored print fabric for the center of the runner*

· *⅓ yard fusible webbing (18" wide) or equivalent*

· *14½" × 34½" piece of low-loft batting or fleece*

· *14½" × 34½" piece of backing fabric of choice*

· *30" of scrap lace, about 1½" wide*

· *All-purpose threads to match all of the fabrics*

For the 9-Block Quilt

· *14½" × 18½" piece of natural solid fabric*

· *¼ yard multicolored print fabric for the borders*

· *Three 6" × 12" pieces of fabric (one each of rust, yellow, and green) for the leaves*

· *⅔ yard fusible webbing (18" wide) or equivalent*

· *21" × 25" piece of low-loft batting or fleece*

· *21" × 25" piece of backing fabric of choice*

· *2½ yards of ½"-wide bias binding (2" wide when unfolded)*

· *All-purpose thread of a neutral color*

· *Fine-point permanent marker*

For the Square Quilt

· *16½" × 16½" square of off-white fabric for the quilt center*

· *Three 6" × 8" pieces of fabric (one each of rust, yellow, and green) for the leaves*

· *⅓ yard multicolored print fabric for the borders*

· *⅓ yard fusible webbing (18" wide) or equivalent*

· *23" × 23" piece of low-loft batting or fleece*

· *23" × 23" piece of backing fabric of choice*

· *All-purpose threads to match all of the fabrics*

· *2½ yards of ½"-wide rust-colored bias binding (2" wide when unfolded)*

The projects in this set work up very quickly and easily. *Finished size of runner: 14" × 34" (plus lace). Finished size of the square quilt: 21" × 21". Finished size of the 9-block quilt: 18" × 22".*

Directions

The appliqué pattern is given without seam allowances (not needed for machine appliqué). Add ¼" seam allowances for hand appliqué. All construction is done with right sides of fabric facing and ¼" seam allowances.

For the Runner

1. Fold each of the off-white 6½" × 14½" strips into thirds and press to mark the folds as shown in Figure 14–1. Trace 6 leaves onto the paper side of the fusible webbing from the leaf pattern and cut them out of the webbing. Fuse two of the leaves to the wrong side of each of the 6" × 8" pieces of fabric (the green, yellow, and rust, and cut them out. Fuse one leaf of each color to each of the off-white 6½" × 14½" strips, centering them between the folds, as shown in Figure 14–2 (see color photo also).

2. Machine-appliqué the leaves in place using matching threads and a medium-width machine satin stitch to make a leaf strip.

3. Stitch one leaf strip to each short end of the multicolored piece of fabric. Baste a length of lace to each short end of the runner front, with raw edges facing out, as shown in Figure 14–3.

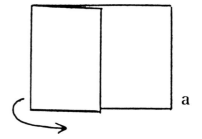

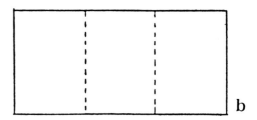

14–1. **a:** *Fold each of the natural strips into thirds and press.* **b:** *The unfolded strip, with crease marks.*

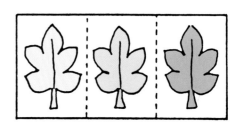

14–2. *Fuse one leaf to each division of the strips, centered on the box.*

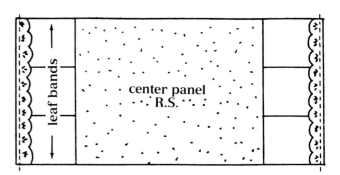

14–3. *Baste the lace to the ends of the runner top, with raw edges out, and aligned with the runner top's raw edges.*

4. Baste the quilt batting to the wrong side of the backing fabric along the edges. With the right side of the quilt front and the right side of the backing fabric facing in, stitch the runner front to the runner backing plus batting, having the raw edges even. Stitch with a ¼" seam allowance, and leave a 4" opening along one long side for turning (Fig. 14–4). Clip the corners of the seam allowances and turn the runner right-side out. Hand-stitch the turning opening closed.

5. Hand- or machine-quilt the runner * as desired to keep the layers from shifting.

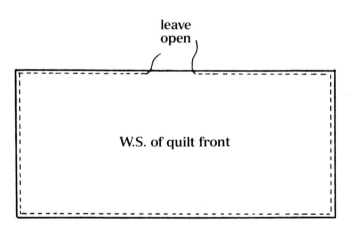

14–4. Stitch around the edges of the runner, leaving a 4" opening for turning along one long edge.

---

*See the quilting pattern section at the back of the book for optional quilting patterns.

For the Square Quilt

1. Fold the 16½" × 16½" off-white square into quarters and press to mark the center (Figure 14–5). Set it aside.

2. Trace 6 leaves from the leaf pattern onto the paper side of the fusible webbing, and cut them out. Fuse two of the leaves to the wrong side of each of the 6" × 8" pieces of fabric (green, yellow and rust), and cut them out. Fuse the leaves to the off-white square of fabric in a circular arrangement around the center, having the ends of the stems 2 inches from the center of the off-white square.

3. Machine-appliqué the leaves in place using threads that match the fabrics and a medium-width machine satin stitch.

4. From the multicolored print fabric, cut two A strips 16½" × 3½" each, and stitch the strips to two opposite sides of the appliquéd center block. Press. Cut two B strips 3½" × 22½" each, and stitch them to the remaining 2 sides (Fig. 14–6). Press.

5. Lay the 23" × 23" backing fabric face down and center the batting over the wrong side of the backing. Center the quilt top over the batting and hand-baste or pin-baste the layers together. Hand- or machine-quilt as desired.

6. Baste all around the quilt top, ¼" from the raw edges, and trim away the excess batting and backing fabric. Bind the edges of the quilt with the bias binding to complete it.

Closeup showing machine appliqué.

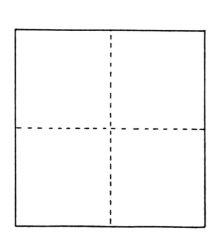

14–5. *Fold the natural square into quarters and press to mark the center.*

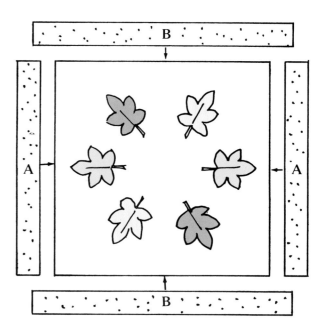

14–6. *Attaching borders to the square quilt.*

For the 9-Block Quilt

The 9-block quilt is "quilted," using the "pen-stitch," with a permanent marker, and has appliqués that are fused in place but not machine-appliquéd (unless you want to sew them in place).

1. Fold the 14½" × 18½" off-white rectangle in thirds lengthwise, as shown in Figure 14–7, and press. Mark along the crease lines with a water-soluble pencil. Fold the piece again into thirds in the opposite direction (Figure 14–8) and press. Mark along these crease lines with pencil as well. You will now have the rectangle divided into 9 equal sections.

2. Trace 9 leaves onto the paper side of fusible webbing and cut them out. Fuse 3 webbing leaves to the wrong side of *each* of the 6" × 12" pieces of fabric (green, rust and yellow). Cut out the leaves, and fuse one leaf to each section of the quilt center (see photo for reference). Make sure they are securely fused, as they aren't going to be appliquéd on.

3. From the print fabric cut two side borders, each 2½" × 18½", and stitch them to the sides of the quilt center using ¼" seam allowances (Fig. 14–9). Cut two more strips, 2½" × 18½" and stitch them to the remaining top and bottom. Press.

4. Lay the 21" × 25" backing fabric face down and center the batting over the wrong side of the backing fabric. Center the quilt top, right-side up, over the batting and pin-baste the layers

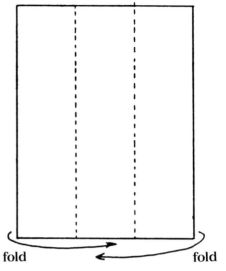

14–7. *Fold the natural rectangle into thirds lengthwise. Press and mark along the crease lines.*

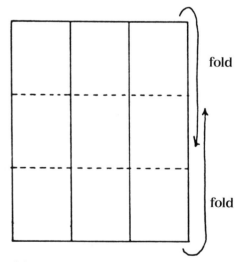

14–8. *Fold the rectangle into thirds widthwise. Press and mark along the crease lines.*

together. Machine-stitch along the seamlines and along the crease lines using natural-colored or invisible thread to keep the layers from shifting.

5. Baste all around the quilt top, ¼" in from the raw edges, and trim away the excess batting and backing fabric. Bind the quilt with the bias binding.

6. Using the permanent pen, mark the pen-stitch around each of the leaves (see Figure 14–10), with the markings approximately ¼" outside of the edges of the leaves. Mark the center vein of the leaves in pen-stitch also. Make marks along the crease lines to delineate the "blocks" of the quilt, to complete.

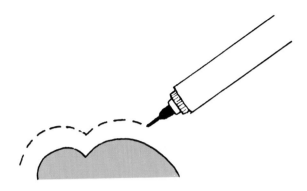

14–10. The pen stitch.

14–9. Attaching borders to the 9-block quilt.

Full-sized leaf pattern. Seam allowances are not included.

Grape Cluster Apron and Bag Set

Materials Required

Apron

- *32½" × 26½" piece of tan print fabric*

- *32½" × 26½" piece of off-white solid fabric for the lining*

- *Scraps of 4 or 5 different purple fabrics, totaling approximately ⅓ yard*

- *¼ yard of dark green print fabric for the leaves*

- *1 yard of fusible transfer webbing (18" wide) or equivalent*

- *⅓ yard of 1"-wide green satin washable ribbon*

- *Fine-line permanent marking pen*

- *Tan all-purpose thread*

- *5 yards of extra-wide double fold bias binding (¼" finished width; 1" wide when opened)*

- *Tan all-purpose sewing thread*

Bottle Bag

- *7½" × 32½" strip of tan print fabric*

- *7½" × 32½" strip of off-white solid fabric for lining*

- *Purple fabric scraps, as for apron*

- *Tan all-purpose sewing thread*

- *1 yard 1"-wide washable green satin ribbon*

- *Scraps of fusible webbing from the apron project*

- *Fine-line permanent marking pen*

This apron and bag set would make a lovely gift for your favorite host or hostess. Don't forget to place a nice bottle of a favorite wine or sparkling beverage in the bag. Finished size of apron, 32½" (length) × 26½" (width). Finished size of bag: 7" × 15". The model uses pen markings (pen stitch) to imitate quilting and simply fuses the grapes and leaves in place. If you prefer to machine appliqué, add green and purple all-purpose thread to your materials list and see the "Basic Techniques" chapter for appliqué instructions.

Directions

All construction is done with ¼" seam allowances.

Apron

1. Enlarge the armhole cutting guide pattern (Fig. 15–1) and use it to trace the armhole curve at the top right and top left corners of the tan 32½" × 26½" piece of fabric (Fig. 15–2). (Flip the pattern over to the left for the left armhole.) Cut the armhole shapes into the tan rectangle; this will be the apron top. Using the apron top as a pattern, cut the armhole shapes into the 32½" × 26½" off-white fabric rectangle as well. Place the lining and apron top together, with right sides facing, and stitch around all the edges EXCEPT the armhole edges (Fig. 15–3). Trim the seam allowances at the bottom corners.

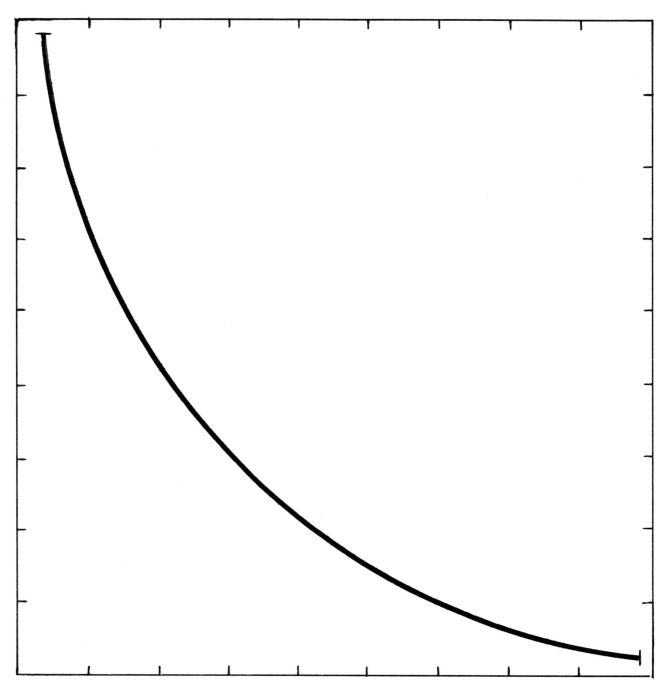

15–1. *Armhole cutting guide pattern for apron. One box = 1". Enlarge pattern (photocopy at 133 percent).*

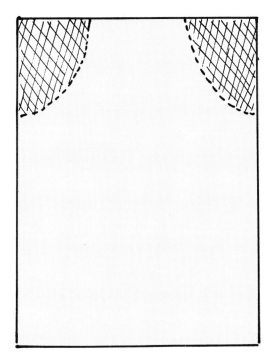

15–2. Cut armhole pieces out of tan fabric. Discard shaded areas.

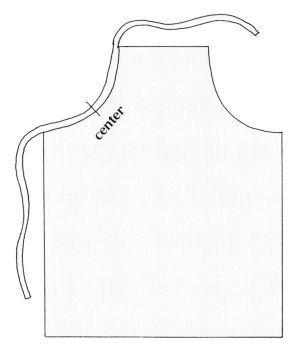

15–4. Align and pin the center of the bias tape to the center of the armhole on the apron back.

15–3. Stitch the apron front to the lining on all edges except the armholes.

2. Turn the apron right-side out through an armhole opening, and press it along all seam lines. Cut the piece of double-fold binding into two equal lengths. Find the center of each piece and mark it.

3. Place the center of the piece of bias tape at the center of each armhole edge on the lining side of the apron, with the right side of the lining facing the right side of the binding, as shown in Figure 15–4. Stitch the binding to the armhole edge along the crease closest to the edge, as shown in Figure 15–5. Fold the binding over to the tan fabric (front) side of the apron, turn under a hem, and stitch it down to the apron. Continue stitching the "tails" of the bias tape closed also, to form the apron strings (Fig. 15–6).

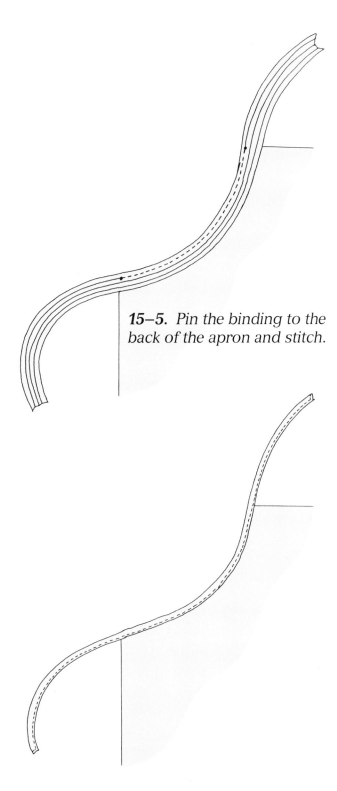

15–5. *Pin the binding to the back of the apron and stitch.*

15–6. *Fold over the raw edges of the binding to the apron front and stitch them down, turning under a hem; stitch the ties closed also.*

15–7. *Suggested arrangement of appliqués for the apron.*

5. Trace 27 grape circles and 3 leaves onto the paper side of the fusible webbing. Cut out the webbing circles and leaves roughly. Fuse the circles to the wrong sides of several colors of purple fabric, and cut them out. Fuse the leaves to the wrong side of the green fabric, and cut them out. Using Figure 15–7 as a model, fuse the leaves and grapes onto the upper front of the apron; or use your own arrangement of leaves and grapes if you prefer. (If you wish, machine appliqué the leaves and grapes in place with matching thread.)

6. After fusing all of the pieces in place, mark around the edges of the appliqués

15–9. *Sew the two sides of the tan bag closed.*

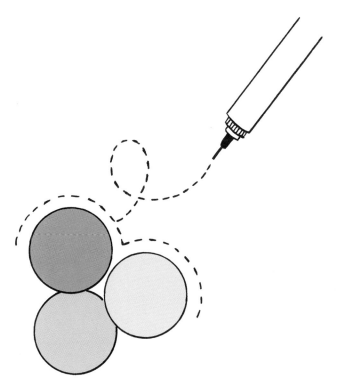

15–8. *Using the permanent pen to do the pen-stitch.*

15–10. *Sew the sides of the lining closed, but leave a turning opening.*

in the "pen stitch," as shown in Figure 15–8. Pen-stitch or machine-appliqué a few vine tendrils (curly lines) to the cluster of grapes if you wish. Tie the green ribbon into a bow and tack it to the apron front by hand.

Bag

1. Fold the tan 7½" × 32½" fabric strip in half to make a 7½" × 16¼" folded piece, with right sides facing, and stitch it along the two long sides, leaving the top (short open) edge unstitched (Fig. 15–9). Repeat with the lining fabric, but also leave a 4" opening along one side for turning (Figure 15–10). Clip the

corners of the seam allowances and turn the tan bag section right-side out. Slip the lining section around the tan bag section so their right sides are facing, and stitch along the top open edge (Fig. 15–11). Turn the bag and lining right-side out through the opening left in the side of the lining.

2. Hand-stitch the lining opening closed. Push the lining into the bag. Press. Stay-stitch along the top edge of the bag as close to the edge as possible, about ⅛" to ¹⁄₁₆" in from the edge (Fig. 15–12).

3. Trace 15 grape circles and 1 leaf onto the bits of fusible webbing remaining from the apron. As you did for the apron, fuse the leaf and the circles to the wrong sides of the green and purple fabrics, and cut them out of the fabrics. Fuse a cluster of grapes to the front of the bag, using Fig. 15–13 as a model, or in another arrangement you like.

4. Mark the lines around the appliqué with pen-stitch, adding a tendril, as for the apron.

5. Insert the bottle into the bag and tie the bag with ribbon around the neck of the bottle.

15–11. *Stitch the bag to the lining at the top.*

15–12. *Stay-stitch the bag to the lining at the top.*

15–13. Suggested arrangement of appliqués for the bag.

Full-size patterns for leaf, grape, and tendril. Seam allowances aren't included; add for hand appliqué only.

Quilting Patterns

Quilting pattern, suitable for Wind Song project.

Quilting pattern, suitable for Wind Song project.

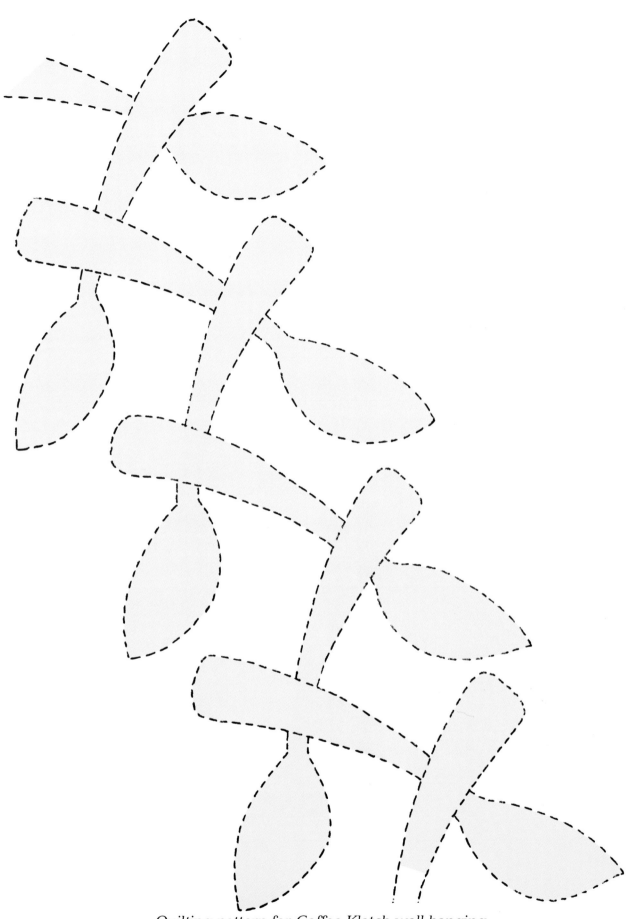

Quilting pattern for Coffee Klatch wall hanging (border).

Quilting pattern for Ships at Sea Baby Quilt.

Quilting pattern for Sunflowers quilt.

Quilting pattern for Baby's Butterflies.

Quilting pattern for Around-the-Square Lap Quilt.

Index

Appliqué, 13–15
Apron, 129–133
Around the Square Lap Quilt, 74–79, 142

Baby's Butterflies, 53–62, 141
Basting the layers, 16
Batting, 23
Bib, 58–62
Binding, 18–21
Birdies' Little Abode Wall Hanging and Pillow, 113–120
Birthday Banner, 91–95
Blanket stitch, 40
Bottle Bag, 133–135
Buttonhole thread, 40

Chain piecing, 11, 12
Checkered strips, 68
Clipping seam allowances, 18
Coaster, 41–42
Coffee Klatch Wall Hanging, 29–36, 138
Confetti Four-Patch Lap Quilt, 86–90
Criss-cross quilting, 17
Curved appliqués, 14, 15

Double-fold bias binding, 19

Echo quilting, 17
Embroidery thread, 26
Even feed foot, 16–17

Fabric, choosing and preparing, 22
Free-motion quilting, 17
Fusible interfacing or webbing, 13, 23

Grape Cluster Apron and Bag Set, 128–135

Hand embroidery, 56
Hand piecing, 11–12
Hand quilting, 17
Hand appliqué, 15, 40
Hanging a quilt, 21

Lace and trim, 15–16, 23
Layers of a quilt, 16
Little Houses Kitchen Set, 37–43
Loft, of batting, 23

Machine appliqué, 14, 23, 25, 40, 47, 56, 98, 125
Machine quilting, 16–17, 58, 83, 125
Masking tape, 26
Metric Equivalents Table, 144

Needles, 26

Other useful items, 26

Paper Dolls Wall Hanging, 102–106
Pens and pencils for marking fabric, 25
Pen-stitch, 127
Pillows, 70, 85, 116
Piping, 15–16
Place mats, 38–40, 49–52
Pressing, 12

Quilting hoops and frames, 25–26
Quilting patterns, 136–142

Rotary cutters, 25
Rows of Roses Wall Hanging and Pillow, 80–85

Satin stitch, 14
Scissors, 25
Seam allowance, 11, 18
Seam ripper, 25
Sewing machine care, 24–25
Ships at Sea Baby Quilt and Pillow, 63–73, 139
Stabilizer, for machine appliqué, 13, 23
Stem stitch, 56
Stepped Star Quilt, 107–112
Stitching guide, 11
Sunflowers Quilt and Place Mat, 44–52, 140

Thimbles, 26
Thread, 11, 13, 22, 16
Triangle (tool), 26
Trim, 15–16

Walking foot, 16–17
Watering Can Wall Hanging, 96–101
Wind Song Lap Quilt and Runner Set, 121–127, 136, 137

Yards Into Inches Table, 144

USEFUL TABLES

A. *Metric Equivalents:*
Inches to Millimetres (mm) and Centimetres (cm)

Inches	mm	cm	Inches	cm	Inches	cm
⅛	3	0.3	9	22.9	30	76.2
¼	6	0.6	10	25.4	31	78.7
⅜	10	1.0	11	27.9	32	81.3
½	13	1.3	12	30.5	33	83.8
⅝	16	1.6	13	33.0	34	86.4
¾	19	1.9	14	35.6	35	88.9
⅞	22	2.2	15	38.1	36	91.4
1	25	2.5	16	40.6	37	94.0
1¼	32	3.2	17	43.2	38	96.5
1½	38	3.8	18	45.7	39	99.1
1¾	44	4.4	19	48.3	40	101.6
2	51	5.1	20	50.8	41	104.1
2½	64	6.4	21	53.3	42	106.7
3	76	7.6	22	55.9	43	109.2
3½	89	8.9	23	58.4	44	111.8
4	102	10.2	24	61.0	45	114.3
4½	114	11.4	25	63.5	46	116.8
5	127	12.7	26	66.0	47	119.4
6	152	15.2	27	68.6	48	121.9
7	178	17.8	28	71.1	49	124.5
8	203	20.3	29	73.7	50	127.0

B. *Yards Into Inches*

Yards	Inches	Yards	Inches
⅛	4.5	1⅛	40.5
¼	9	1¼	45
⅜	13.5	1⅜	49.5
½	18	1½	54
⅝	22.5	1⅝	58.5
¾	27	1¾	63
⅞	31.5	1⅞	67.5
1	36	2	72